THE ENCYCLOPEDIA OF PSYCHOACTIVE DRUGS

SERIES 1

The Addictive Personality
Alcohol and Alcoholism
Alcohol Customs and Rituals
Alcohol Teenage Drinking
Amphetamines Danger in the Fast Lane
Barbiturates Sleeping Potion or Intoxicant?
Caffeine The Most Popular Stimulant
Cocaine A New Epidemic
Escape from Anxiety and Stress
Flowering Plants Magic in Bloom
Getting Help Treatments for Drug Abuse
Heroin The Street Narcotic
Inhalants The Toxic Fumes

LSD Visions or Nightmares?
Marijuana Its Effects on Mind & Body
Methadone Treatment for Addiction
Mushrooms Psychedelic Fungi
Nicotine An Old-Fashioned Addiction
Over-The-Counter Drugs Harmless or Hazardous?
PCP The Dangerous Angel
Prescription Narcotics The Addictive Painkillers
Quaaludes The Quest for Oblivion
Teenage Depression and Drugs
Treating Mental Illness
Valium The Tranquil Trap

SERIES 2

Bad Trips
Brain Function
Case Histories
Celebrity Drug Use
Designer Drugs
The Downside of Drugs
Drinking, Driving, and Drugs
Drugs and Civilization
Drugs and Crime
Drugs and Diet
Drugs and Disease
Drugs and Emotion
Drugs and Pain
Drugs and Perception
Drugs and Pregnancy
Drugs and Sexual Behavior

Drugs and Sleep
Drugs and Sports
Drugs and the Arts
Drugs and the Brain
Drugs and the Family
Drugs and the Law
Drugs and Women
Drugs of the Future
Drugs Through the Ages
Drug Use Around the World
Legalization A Debate
Mental Disturbances
Nutrition and the Brain
The Origins and Sources of Drugs
Substance Abuse Prevention and Cures
Who Uses Drugs?

CASE HISTORIES

GENERAL EDITOR

Professor Solomon H. Snyder, M.D.

*Distinguished Service Professor of
Neuroscience, Pharmacology, and Psychiatry at
The Johns Hopkins University School of Medicine*

•

ASSOCIATE EDITOR

Professor Barry L. Jacobs, Ph.D.

*Program in Neuroscience, Department of Psychology,
Princeton University*

•

SENIOR EDITORIAL CONSULTANT

Joann Rodgers

*Deputy Director, Office of Public Affairs at
The Johns Hopkins Medical Institutions*

SOLOMON H. SNYDER, M.D. • GENERAL EDITOR

THE ENCYCLOPEDIA OF PSYCHOACTIVE DRUGS

SERIES 2

CASE HISTORIES

DIANNE HALES

CHELSEA HOUSE PUBLISHERS

NEW YORK • NEW HAVEN • PHILADELPHIA

EDITOR-IN-CHIEF: Nancy Toff
EXECUTIVE EDITOR: Remmel T. Nunn
MANAGING EDITOR: Karyn Gullen Browne
COPY CHIEF: Juliann Barbato
ART DIRECTOR: Giannella Garrett
MANUFACTURING MANAGER: Gerald Levine

Staff For CASE HISTORIES:

SENIOR EDITOR: Jane Larkin Crain
ASSOCIATE EDITOR: Paula Edelson
ASSISTANT EDITOR: Michele A. Merens
EDITORIAL ASSISTANT: Laura-Ann Dolce
COPYEDITORS: Sean Dolan, Gillian Bucky, Ellen Scordato
PICTURE EDITOR: Juliette Dickstein
ILLUSTRATOR: Nava Atlas
DESIGNER: Victoria Tomaselli
PRODUCTION COORDINATOR: Laura McCormick
COVER ILLUSTRATION: Betsy Scheld

CREATIVE DIRECTOR: Harold Steinberg

Library of Congress Cataloging-in-Publication Data

Hales, Dianne R., 1950–
   Case histories.

   (The Encyclopedia of psychoactive drugs. Series 2)
   Bibliography: p.
   Includes index.
   1. Substance abuse—Case studies—Juvenile literature.
I. Title. II. Series.
RC564.H35   1987   362.2′9   87-526

ISBN 1-55546-217-0

CONTENTS

DRUG FREE

Phoenix House

A poster for Phoenix House, a New York City rehabilitation center. Treatment facilities providing a variety of therapies are located in every state for addicts seeking both immediate and long-term help.

FOREWORD

In the Mainstream
of American Life

One of the legacies of the social upheaval of the 1960s is that psychoactive drugs have become part of the mainstream of American life. Schools, homes, and communities cannot be "drug proofed." There is a demand for drugs — and the supply is plentiful. Social norms have changed and drugs are not only available—they are everywhere.

But where efforts to curtail the supply of drugs and outlaw their use have had tragically limited effects on demand, it may be that education has begun to stem the rising tide of drug abuse among young people and adults alike.

Over the past 25 years, as drugs have become an increasingly routine facet of contemporary life, a great many teenagers have adopted the notion that drug taking was somehow a right or a privilege or a necessity. They have done so, however, without understanding the consequences of drug use during the crucial years of adolescence.

The teenage years are few in the total life cycle, but critical in the maturation process. During these years adolescents face the difficult tasks of discovering their identity, clarifying their sexual roles, asserting their independence, learning to cope with authority, and searching for goals that will give their lives meaning.

Drugs rob adolescents of precious time, stamina, and health. They interrupt critical learning processes, sometimes forever. Teenagers who use drugs are likely to withdraw increasingly into themselves, to "cop out" at just the time when they most need to reach out and experience the world.

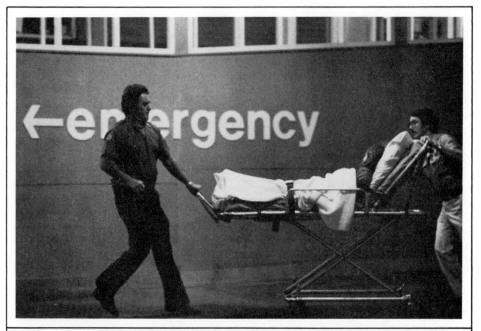

The effects of drugs differ from person to person. A dosage that is tolerable for one user can be dangerous, or even fatal, to another.

Fortunately, as a recent Gallup poll shows, young people are beginning to realize this, too. They themselves label drugs their most important problem. In the last few years, moreover, the climate of tolerance and ignorance surrounding drugs has been changing.

Adolescents as well as adults are becoming aware of mounting evidence that every race, ethnic group, and class is vulnerable to drug dependency.

Recent publicity about the cost and failure of drug rehabilitation efforts; dangerous drug use among pilots, air traffic controllers, star athletes, and Hollywood celebrities; and drug-related accidents, suicides, and violent crime have focused the public's attention on the need to wage an all-out war on drug abuse before it seriously undermines the fabric of society itself.

The anti-drug message is getting stronger and there is evidence that the message is beginning to get through to adults and teenagers alike.

The Encyclopedia of Psychoactive Drugs hopes to play a part in the national campaign now underway to educate young people about drugs. Series 1 provides clear and comprehensive discussions of common psychoactive substances, outlines their psychological and physiological effects on the mind and body, explains how they "hook" the user, and separates fact from myth in the complex issue of drug abuse.

Whereas Series 1 focuses on specific drugs, such as nicotine or cocaine, Series 2 confronts a broad range of both social and physiological phenomena. Each volume addresses the ramifications of drug use and abuse on some aspect of human experience: social, familial, cultural, historical, and physical. Separate volumes explore questions about the effects of drugs on brain chemistry and unborn children; the use and abuse of painkillers; the relationship between drugs and sexual behavior, sports, and the arts; drugs and disease; the role of drugs in history; and the sophisticated drugs now being developed in the laboratory that will profoundly change the future.

Each book in the series is fully illustrated and is tailored to the needs and interests of young readers. The more adolescents know about drugs and their role in society, the less likely they are to misuse them.

Joann Rodgers
Senior Editorial Consultant

Edvard Munch's classic woodcut The Scream *epitomizes for many the desperation and helplessness of the drug addict.*

INTRODUCTION

The Gift of Wizardry
Use and Abuse

JACK H. MENDELSON, M.D.
NANCY K. MELLO, Ph.D.
Alcohol and Drug Abuse Research Center
Harvard Medical School—McLean Hospital

Dorothy to the Wizard:

"I think you are a very bad man," said Dorothy.
"Oh no, my dear; I'm really a very good man; but I'm a very bad Wizard."

—from THE WIZARD OF OZ

Man is endowed with the gift of wizardry, a talent for discovery and invention. The discovery and invention of substances that change the way we feel and behave are among man's special accomplishments, and, like so many other products of our wizardry, these substances have the capacity to harm as well as to help. Psychoactive drugs can cause profound changes in the chemistry of the brain and other vital organs, and although their legitimate use can relieve pain and cure disease, their abuse leads in a tragic number of cases to destruction.

Consider alcohol — available to all and yet regarded with intense ambivalence from biblical times to the present day. The use of alcoholic beverages dates back to our earliest ancestors. Alcohol use and misuse became associated with the worship of gods and demons. One of the most powerful Greek gods was Dionysus, lord of fruitfulness and god of wine. The Romans adopted Dionysus but changed his name to Bacchus. Festivals and holidays associated with Bacchus celebrated the harvest and the origins of life. Time has blurred the images of the Bacchanalian festival, but the theme of drunkenness as a major part of celebration has survived the pagan gods and remains a familiar part of modern society. The term "Bacchanalian Festival" conveys a more appealing image than "drunken orgy" or "pot party," but whatever the label, drinking alcohol is a form of drug use that results in addiction for millions.

The fact that many millions of other people can use alcohol in moderation does not mitigate the toll this drug takes on society as a whole. According to reliable estimates, one out of every ten Americans develops a serious alcohol-related problem sometime in his or her lifetime. In addition, automobile accidents caused by drunken drivers claim the lives of tens of thousands every year. Many of the victims are gifted young people, just starting out in adult life. Hospital emergency rooms abound with patients seeking help for alcohol-related injuries.

Who is to blame? Can we blame the many manufacturers who produce such an amazing variety of alcoholic beverages? Should we blame the educators who fail to explain the perils of intoxication, or so exaggerate the dangers of drinking that no one could possibly believe them? Are friends to blame — those peers who urge others to "drink more and faster," or the macho types who stress the importance of being able to "hold your liquor"? Casting blame, however, is hardly constructive, and pointing the finger is a fruitless way to deal with the problem. Alcoholism and drug abuse have few culprits but many victims. Accountability begins with each of us, every time we choose to use or misuse an intoxicating substance.

It is ironic that some of man's earliest medicines, derived from natural plant products, are used today to poison and to intoxicate. Relief from pain and suffering is one of society's many continuing goals. Over 3,000 years ago, the Therapeutic Papyrus of Thebes, one of our earliest written records, gave instructions for the use of opium in the treatment of pain. Opium, in the form of its major derivative, morphine, and similar compounds, such as heroin, have also been used by many to induce changes in mood and feeling. Another example of man's misuse of a natural substance is the coca leaf, which for centuries was used by the Indians of Peru to reduce fatigue and hunger. Its modern derivative, cocaine, has important medical use as a local anesthetic. Unfortunately, its increasing abuse in the 1980s clearly has reached epidemic proportions.

The purpose of this series is to explore in depth the psychological and behavioral effects that psychoactive drugs have on the individual, and also, to investigate the ways in which drug use influences the legal, economic, cultural, and even moral aspects of societies. The information presented here (and in other books in this series) is based on many clinical and laboratory studies and other observations by people from diverse walks of life.

Over the centuries, novelists, poets, and dramatists have provided us with many insights into the sometimes seductive but ultimately problematic aspects of alcohol and drug use. Physicians, lawyers, biologists, psychologists, and social scientists have contributed to a better understanding of the causes and consequences of using these substances. The authors in this series have attempted to gather and condense all the latest information about drug use and abuse. They have also described the sometimes wide gaps in our knowledge and have suggested some new ways to answer many difficult questions.

One such question, for example, is how do alcohol and drug problems get started? And what is the best way to treat them when they do? Not too many years ago, alcoholics and drug abusers were regarded as evil, immoral, or both. It is now recognized that these persons suffer from very complicated diseases involving deep psychological and social problems. To understand how the disease begins and progresses, it is necessary to understand the nature of the substance, the behavior of addicts, and the characteristics of the society or culture in which they live.

Although many of the social environments we live in are very similar, some of the most subtle differences can strongly influence our thinking and behavior. Where we live, go to school and work, whom we discuss things with — all influence our opinions about drug use and misuse. Yet we also share certain commonly accepted beliefs that outweigh any differences in our attitudes. The authors in this series have tried to identify and discuss the central, most crucial issues concerning drug use and misuse.

Despite the increasing sophistication of the chemical substances we create in the laboratory, we have a long way to go in our efforts to make these powerful drugs work for us rather than against us.

The volumes in this series address a wide range of timely questions. What influence has drug use had on the arts? Why do so many of today's celebrities and star athletes use drugs, and what is being done to solve this problem? What is the relationship between drugs and crime? What is the physiological basis for the power drugs can hold over us? These are but a few of the issues explored in this far-ranging series.

Educating people about the dangers of drugs can go a long way towards minimizing the desperate consequences of substance abuse for individuals and society as a whole. Luckily, human beings have the resources to solve even the most serious problems that beset them, once they make the commitment to do so. As one keen and sensitive observer, Dr. Lewis Thomas, has said,

> There is nothing at all absurd about the human condition. We matter. It seems to me a good guess, hazarded by a good many people who have thought about it, that we may be engaged in the formation of something like a mind for the life of this planet. If this is so, we are still at the most primitive stage, still fumbling with language and thinking, but infinitely capacitated for the future. Looked at this way, it is remarkable that we've come as far as we have in so short a period, really no time at all as geologists measure time. We are the newest, youngest, and the brightest thing around.

CASE
HISTORIES

AUTHOR'S PREFACE

A high-school cheerleader in Dallas. A factory worker in Detroit. A stockbroker in San Francisco. A professional ball player in Kansas City. A young mother in Atlanta. A varsity track star in Phoenix. A rock singer in Los Angeles. A college sophomore in Boston. A street kid in the South Bronx. A ballerina in New York City.

Some of these people are celebrities, with famous faces and names; most are not. Some are barely in their teens; others are parents of teenagers. They come from all ethnic backgrounds, races, religions, and political groups. And all share a common problem: drugs.

The sheer number of Americans using drugs is staggering. About 20 million smoke marijuana regularly; 500,000 are heroin addicts. Roughly 24 million — about one out of every ten Americans — have used cocaine; every day, more than 5,000 people try it for the first time. By the time they reach their middle twenties, as many as 80% of young adults have used an illegal drug.

But the statistics just begin to reveal the problem. These figures represent real people, each one brimming with dreams and desires, each one desperately wanting to be happy or, at least, happier.

This book tells the stories of ten such people — men, women, and teens. Although names and circumstances have been changed to protect privacy, every incident is based on fact. The people described in this book never thought they would become addicts or alcoholics. "It'll never happen to me," they told themselves. "I'll never get hooked. I'm too smart, too lucky. I know too much about drugs."

But getting hooked on drugs is not a matter of being smart or lucky. Drugs are sophisticated chemicals. Once in the human body, they slowly take command. By the time a user realizes what has happened, it is too late. The drugs are in control.

The process is almost always the same. There is a definite pattern in these case histories, particularly among the teen-agers. Research reveals that young people between the ages of 14 and 24 are the most likely to experiment with drugs. Why? Some are simply curious or bored. Often friends offer them drugs, and they do not know how to say no. They want to belong, rebel, or explore something new and intriguing.

The first time a teen lights a marijuana joint, takes a pill, tries cocaine, or gets drunk, it does not seem like a big event. But the first time can lead to a second, and a third. Eventually even those who swore they would never use drugs may enter what mental health professionals call "Stage One" of drug dependency.

In this stage, novice users discover a new language, new hangouts, new friends, and a new feeling. For many, the "high" that chemicals such as alcohol or marijuana induce is a sur-prising, seductive sensation. But they use drugs only at parties or a friend's house. They think that if they stay straight during the week, they will not get into trouble.

In "Stage Two," users are no longer content to wait for an offer to share a high. They begin to beg for or buy drugs, especially when they are under stress. They are convinced that marijuana or alcohol makes it easier to cope with dis-appointments, such as not making a team or failing a test.

At this stage, their behavior begins to change: they drop out of sports or extracurricular activities and hang out only with their new drug-taking friends. Schoolwork slips. Many try other drugs, such as inhalants, hashish, or amphetamines. Often sexual exploration accompanies drug experimentation.

As they start to lead double lives, young users seesaw from the thrill of trying the forbidden to feelings of shame and guilt. Drugs no longer make them feel good. They suffer hangovers or mild withdrawal. To handle their growing psychological and physical discomfort, they turn again to chemical answers, using drugs on their own as well as with others on weekends. At this point they are "hooked." By the end of Stage Two, there is little, if any, hope of turning back without outside help.

In "Stage Three," users are preoccupied with getting high. Their behavior at school and home is unpredictable and unsettling. They get into fights with parents, teachers, and friends. Because increasing amounts of drugs are costing them more money, they start stealing or dealing, often ending up in trouble with the police. Depressed, guilty, even suicidal, they seek chemical comfort from other drugs, such as LSD or cocaine.

Meanwhile, a teenager's family may start to fall apart. One parent, usually the mother, may feel guilty for not providing enough love and understanding. Angry and frustrated, the father may insist on stricter rules and more discipline. Blaming each other, parents hope their child's behavior is only a phase. They often refuse to admit, even to themselves, that drugs are the real issue.

In "Stage Four," denying the problem becomes impossible for teens and their families. The users either drop out or flunk out of school. They try any drug they can get and do almost anything for a high. They are living to use drugs and using drugs to live. The psychological and physical pain of daily life is too much for them to bear without chemicals. Drugs are the focus of every waking moment of their lives.

Physically, drugs take a terrible toll. Heavy users become fatigued, cough constantly, lose weight, and ache from head to toe. They suffer blackouts, flashbacks, and episodes of increasingly bizarre behavior, often triggered by escalating paranoia. Their risk of overdose rises steadily. Deep down they may yearn to change, but they cannot — not until they are drug free. Their drug dependence has taken over their lives.

Yet, as the stories in this volume show, even individuals who have been addicts for years can and do recover. The best time to seek help, mental health professionals agree, is as soon as a chemical begins to affect the way a person acts or thinks, rather than after complete physical and psychological dependence develops.

Treatment of drug abuse is never easy, and the path to recovery is long and hard. Usually the first step is *detoxification* (supervised withdrawal from drugs, either with or without medication, often in a hospital). The intensity and duration of withdrawal depends on the nature and extent of a user's addiction.

After cleansing their bodies of drugs, many former users participate in treatment programs that include intensive individual and group counseling. Because their lives once revolved around the process of obtaining drugs, they have substituted chemicals for human relationships. After they overcome their physical dependence, they have to rebuild a network of personal contacts in their daily lives.

To do this, teenagers may spend months away from home and their drug-using friends in "therapeutic communities," where they must follow strict rules and earn the right to privileges, such as a phone call to their parents. Users of all ages often find lifelong support in groups, such as Narcotics Anonymous or Alcoholics Anonymous, which help them live without chemicals one day at a time.

No one treatment is right for all drug users. "There are different forms because there are different types of people," says psychiatrist John Talbott, M.D., who is the chairman of psychiatry at the University of Maryland and a former president of the American Psychiatric Association. "It's not that any one of them is good or bad, but that they are good for some and bad for others."

The various forms of drug treatment can and do work. In a five-year follow-up study of patients from Phoenix House, a therapeutic community in New York City that treats many hard-core addicts, more than 75% of the former patients were not using drugs, were not in trouble with the law, and were in school or employed full time. Many other programs, which treat clients with addictions that are often not as severe as those at Phoenix House, report success rates of 80% to 90%.

Most of the stories in this book are tales of triumph rather than tragedy. Slowly, painfully, these individuals reclaimed control over their minds, bodies, and lives. Their experiences are testimony, not to the power of drugs, but to the power of the human spirit and to the promise of a brighter future without drugs.

CHAPTER 1

JIMMY: UNDER THE INFLUENCE

Little Jimmy Turner's father always let him have a sip of his beer. Jimmy would giggle as the bubbles fizzed up his nose. His father's pals would laugh and offer him more from their bottles. Jimmy loved being the center of attention. And he sort of liked the funny way the beer made him feel.

When he was seven, Jimmy slipped into a party a teenager in his Seattle neighborhood was giving. There he asked a much older girl to dance. She laughed and told him to come back in 10 years. Jimmy felt his face redden as the laughter spread. He had never been so humiliated. Running home, he dashed into the kitchen and, for the first time, opened a can of beer on his own and drank it down. The familiar fizzy feeling helped soothe the ache inside.

Jimmy kept drinking on and off through junior high school. What amazed him was how easy it was. His father was always drinking beer, so no one noticed when a few extra cans were missing. When he switched to hard liquor, taking it from the bar in the family room, his parents did not notice anything amiss; liquor flowed so freely in their home no one really kept track.

"God, are they dumb!" Jimmy would think as he tucked a flask into his jacket. At school he would stash vodka in his locker. His friends knew what he was doing, but no one ever said anything. "I guess nobody cares," he thought, taking another swig. "Maybe they think I'm cool."

In high school Jimmy began using other drugs, primarily marijuana. With some other boys, he would slip out of study hall and share a joint. By his junior year he was dozing off in classes. Nothing could hold his interest — not school, sports, girls, or cars.

At home Jimmy became increasingly belligerent. If his parents asked him a question, he would go into a rage and hurl obscenities at them. Shocked and worried, they insisted that Jimmy go with them to a family therapy center. The counselor, who never asked Jimmy if he used drugs or alcohol, listened with a bored expression and assured Jimmy's parents that he was going through a stage and would outgrow his rebelliousness soon enough. Jimmy had to force himself not to laugh.

One night he tried something new: marijuana laced with PCP, a powerful hallucinogen. Suddenly he began screaming and running through the house. Grabbing a knife in the kitchen, he slashed madly at his father, who barely managed to kick the knife out of Jimmy's hand.

"It was like a scene in a bad movie," Jimmy's mother recalled later. "But my husband and my son were in it, not some Hollywood actors. I was screaming. They were screaming. It was insane."

Jimmy's father wrestled the boy to the floor and held him there while his mother called an ambulance. The paramedics strapped Jimmy to a stretcher and took him to a hospital. As the drugs left his body over the next several hours, Jimmy remembered hallucinating that his father was the devil. His parents had him admitted to a hospital psychiatric ward.

But Jimmy soon convinced the staff and his parents that he had just started using drugs. He swore he would try to behave better. "No more PCP," Jimmy told himself. "I'll stick to booze."

The next year was a nightmare for the entire Turner family. They no longer sat down to dinner together. There had been too many confrontations, too many broken dishes and hateful words. Everyone lived in fear of what Jimmy might do next.

Jimmy's outbursts grew more frequent. His parents were afraid to go out because they did not know what they would find when they came home; once he smashed his mother's prized crystal on the dining-room floor. They were afraid to invite people over, apprehensive about what he might do or say during their visit.

Jimmy's 12-year-old sister, Tamara, cringed as he raged through the house. "Why can't we be like normal people?" she asked her mother. "I hate Jimmy. I hate what he's done to us." Jimmy's father worked later and later, trying to postpone the dreaded moment when he had to go home and put his key in the door at night. His mother relied on tranquilizers to make it through the day and ease her way into sleep at night. His parents rarely talked about anything but Jimmy.

"How can you chat about the weather when your own son is destroying himself in front of you?" his father asked. "We ate, walked, and talked Jimmy, always trying to figure out what we'd done wrong, why he'd turned out this way."

The Turner house became a battlefield in a tense war of nerves. When his parents refused to give Jimmy money, he turned up the volume of his stereo and blasted them with rock music all night long. Pushed beyond their limits of patience, they wondered whether they should force him to leave. But they were afraid to throw him out.

One of their friends had locked her 16-year-old son out of the house after years of drug use and disruptive behavior. "This is my birthday present to me!" she had shouted at him. A few nights later the boy got a shotgun and fired it into his mouth outside his mother's house. A note in his pocket read, "Here's my present to you."

But when Tamara became withdrawn and depressed and began doing badly in school, the Turners decided they had had enough. Unwilling to sacrifice one child for another, they readmitted Jimmy to a psychiatric hospital. Badly shaken by how out-of-control his life had become, Jimmy finally agreed to make a serious try at drug rehabilitation.

The treatment program in which Jimmy enrolled involved his living at the facility where it was administered. There were strict rules and guidelines; each patient was expected to adhere to those regulations and take responsibility for his or her own actions.

From the very beginning, the rest of the Turner family was also involved. They learned about chemical dependency and its various stages. In several counseling sessions, they gathered with other people close to Jimmy — some teachers, his swimming coach, and his old friends — and talked about how they felt toward Jimmy, revealing not only care and concern, but also years of buried anger and resentment.

After a few such meetings, this group, along with a counselor, confronted Jimmy to let him know how they felt about him and his sickness. Each person listed two or three specific incidents involving Jimmy's behavior.

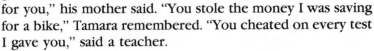

"You were too drunk to go to school, and I had to lie for you," his mother said. "You stole the money I was saving for a bike," Tamara remembered. "You cheated on every test I gave you," said a teacher.

At first Jimmy was furious. He thought they were ganging up on him. But slowly he began to hear the message between the lines, the sense of caring and love. In effect his family and friends were saying, "We know you have a disease, and we know what it has been making you do and feel." By the time each person had spoken, Jimmy could not deny the overwhelming evidence that he had a drinking problem.

"You're right," he said, and began to sob. "I need help." Jimmy felt strangely relieved. Someone else had finally taken charge. Someone had cared enough to force him to stop.

As part of his treatment, Jimmy learned about drug abuse and its effects on mind, body, family, friends, and schoolwork. His days at the center were busy and full: he had to keep up with class work, participate in group therapy, take on simple responsibilities, write essays on drug dependence, and define his personal recovery goals. If he performed well, he earned the privilege of calling his parents once a week.

After a few weeks Jimmy was asked to write down his feelings toward his family. They did the same. After reading each other's words, they went through a process called "amends," in which each person said what he or she was most sorry for.

"I'm sorry I never told you how much I love you," Jimmy's father said, his voice breaking. Suddenly father and son were in each other's arms, saying words never spoken out loud in the past.

"Why didn't you ever tell me before?" Jimmy asked. His stunned father replied that he thought Jimmy knew how much he cared. "Why would I do all I do for you if I didn't love you? Why would I bother?" he asked.

During the second phase of the treatment program, the emphasis shifted from understanding Jimmy's drug-filled past to preparing for a drug-free future. Jimmy began a regular exercise program and learned relaxation techniques to reduce tension. He attended lectures on sexuality and values and also started taking on more responsibility at the center.

In the third phase, Jimmy slowly reentered the community. Switching schools, he made new friends and found a part-time job. He learned how to budget his time and keep his promises to others. For a few weeks, Jimmy lived with another family whose child had abused drugs. There he could relate to the adults without the tension he remembered between him and his parents. By talking with his hosts, he began to see his parents' perspective and understand their sense of helplessness.

Jimmy finally returned to a very different home from the one he had left. The Turners themselves had stopped drinking. They continued to attend a support group for parents, just as he continued to attend a self-help group for teenage alcoholics. And they talked to each other constantly, expressing their feelings rather than bottling them up inside.

"Before we were a bunch of unhappy people with the same address," his mother says. "Now we're a family."

CHAPTER 2

JENNIFER:
ALL IN THE FAMILY

Jennifer did not cry at her brother's funeral. She was too angry. She could see her father's clenched jaw and hear her mother's choking sobs. Mike's classmates were all red-eyed. Tears slid down his teachers' cheeks. Even the minister broke down during the eulogy.

"But it's all his fault!" Jennifer wanted to scream. "Mike didn't have to die. He let it happen to him." She knew she would never forgive him for leaving her, for hurting her the way he did.

Jennifer knew Mike was doing drugs long before their parents ever suspected. Years ago, when she was just nine and playing in his room, she had found half a dozen small vodka bottles stacked behind his desk. He was furious at her for poking around his room. Because she worshipped her 12-year-old brother, Jennifer swore she would never tell.

Later, when she found the tiny plastic bags of what looked like dried-up grass, she did not say a word, not even to Mike. But she knew that they were the real reason why Mike and their parents were always screaming at each other. "Be nice. Please be nice," she would say to all of them, throwing her arms around their necks.

When she started high school at 13, Jennifer was shocked to hear some older kids describe Mike, then 16, as a "druggie." But she knew they were right. Although Mike locked the door to his room, she had glimpsed the pills and packets he slipped in and out of his pockets.

Jennifer wanted to talk to someone about it — to Mike, to her parents — but she did not know where to start. They lived in a small town in Massachusetts, where all the families knew each other. The adults acted as if drugs were a big-city problem, one that could never touch them or their children.

Jennifer was sure that her parents either did not know or did not want to know that Mike was on drugs. The ugly arguments had stopped. Now Mike and their parents rarely even spoke. They seemed to have given up. Maybe they were hoping Mike would suddenly go back to being the way he once was. Jennifer hoped so, too.

Late one night, Jennifer woke up to hear the phone ringing. There was a brief silence as the phone was answered, then her mother's anguished cry, "No!" By the time the family got to the hospital, Mike was dead.

Jennifer overheard the police talking: Mike had been driving their father's car at 95 miles an hour when he crashed through the guardrail and into a ravine. The car was crushed. It took the rescue team an hour just to pry Mike and his girl friend out of the wreckage. The girl was dead. Mike hung on for a few more hours.

"Stoned out of his mind," one of the officers said. "Poor, dumb kid."

In the months after Mike's death, those words haunted Jennifer. Mike was not poor, and he was not dumb. Then why was he dead? Why? Jennifer decided to talk to some of Mike's friends. Maybe they had the answers. She began to spend time with them.

The first time Mike's friend Bob offered her some marijuana, she got angry. "That's what killed Mike," she snapped. But the more she thought about Mike, the more she wondered what it was about drugs that he had liked so much. Maybe the only way she would ever understand would be to try them herself. Soon she did.

Jennifer never thought she would start using drugs. She did not even enjoy the way drinking beer or smoking marijuana made her feel. But she loved being with Mike's friends. The more time she spent with them, the closer she felt to her brother.

Jennifer began to understand why Mike had not been able to get along with their parents. Now they seemed to be displeased with her all the time. She started to feel the same way he had about school—that it was a waste of time.

Just as Mike once did, Jennifer began to stay out past her curfew and ignore her parents' threats and lectures. "It's my life," she would shout. "I'm entitled to do what I want with it." And what she wanted to do was be with Mike's friends. They were introducing her to new drugs, such as hashish and LSD, and she was spending more and more time getting high.

She became a skillful liar. When her parents asked where she was going, she would have one of her drug-using friends call, pretending to be a classmate's mother. Once Jennifer's father insisted on driving her to the house where she said she was staying with a girl friend for the night. He drove away as she rang the bell, so he did not see a stranger answer the door. With a giggle, Jennifer explained that she had the wrong address and ran off to meet her friends.

But even when Jennifer was successful in such deceptions, her parents knew that something was wrong. This time they were not willing to stand by and watch. "We've lost one child," they told her one evening. "We're not going to lose another." They gave her two choices: to enter a drug treatment program or leave home.

Jennifer left. She stayed with a friend for a night. She spent another at a bus station, trying to work up the nerve to buy a one-way ticket to New York City. When she finally reached for her wallet, it was gone. She had been robbed.

Frightened, hungry, and exhausted, Jennifer went home. "I'll do anything you want," she said, "but don't send me to a hospital." Her parents refused. She would have to get help if she wanted to come home. Jennifer nodded her head in agreement, but she refused to say another word.

At the private hospital they had chosen, Jennifer continued her silent strategy. They could force her to stay, she figured, but they could not force her to do anything else.

"You don't have to talk," one of the doctors finally told her. "But that means you won't get any privileges, and you'll end up staying here a lot longer. It's up to you."

For three days Jennifer sulked in her room. Then she decided to go to one of the therapy groups just to see what it was like. After two weeks of listening to other kids — kids just like her — talk about their drug problems and their families, she began to open up a little.

Talking was easier than she had thought. No one criticized her. No one made her feel bad. Encouraged to explore her feelings, Jennifer began to talk more openly each day. After three weeks in the hospital, she felt ready to see her parents again. They were awkward at first, not touching, not looking at each other. Slowly, they began to speak. But when they started talking about Mike, Jennifer became enraged.

"You let it happen," she screamed. "You had to know what was going on. He was doing dope for years, and you didn't do a thing about it. You let him die!"

She ran to her room, refusing to talk to anyone. That night she wandered the halls, trying to find something to ease her pain. The night watchman found her trying to break into the pharmacy. She lost all her privileges. After two more days of sulking, Jennifer admitted she was wrong. The counselors praised her for taking responsibility for her actions.

The following week Jennifer talked about Mike in group therapy. She remembered how he used to toss her in the air when she was little, how he would tease and tickle her, how he taught her to ride a bike. As she talked about how he had changed when he started using drugs, the tears finally came. She sobbed and sobbed, surrounded by other teens who genuinely seemed to understand her pain.

The next week Jennifer met with her parents again. There were more tears, but this time the family clung to each other, letting the pain out, saying they loved each other, sharing their grief over Mike's death.

Ten weeks after she entered the hospital, Jennifer went home. With the staff's help she and her parents wrote a contract, then each family member signed it. In it, Jennifer agreed not to use drugs, to associate only with friends from the drug-abuse program, to attend group sessions three times a week, to maintain at least a B average at school, and to complete chores at home, such as cleaning up after dinner and washing the car every week.

Jennifer's parents agreed to attend a family therapy session with her every week, to drive her to and from her meetings, not to drink at home, and not to ground her without discussion in family therapy. For keeping up her part of the bargain, Jennifer would be able to stay out until 10:30 P.M. on weekend nights, provided her parents knew that she was with non-drug-using friends.

If she "slipped," she would be grounded for a month. If she slipped a second time, she might have to return to the hospital. "Don't worry," Jennifer promised, "there won't be any slips."

After eight weeks, Jennifer and her parents renegotiated the contract, providing her with more privileges as well as a weekly allowance. For six months after her return home, they continued their weekly family therapy sessions.

A year later, Jennifer still attends one group meeting a week, but she feels that she has left what she calls "my druggie stage" behind. She is making plans for college and a career in computer science after that. "I still miss Mike," she says. "For a while I thought drugs could keep me close to him. Now I know better."

35

CHAPTER 3

DAVID: "IT'S ONLY POT"

When other parents complained about their teenagers, Sam and Linda Marks would look at each other and smile. "Thank God, David's not like that," they would say to each other. "We're so lucky."

David had always been a "perfect" son, bright and eager to please. With an IQ of 142, he earned straight As and ranked at the top of his class. He was planning to become a doctor, like his father. "You'll be the partner I always wanted," his father would say.

When he turned 16, David started an accelerated science program to qualify for advanced placement courses in college. Accustomed to breezing through his course work, David felt swamped. For the first time in his life, his grades slipped from As to Bs.

"Maybe I won't get into a good college," he thought, worried. "Maybe I can't make it in premed." All his life his parents had praised and rewarded David for doing well in school. He was not good at sports. He did not have many friends. He felt uncomfortable around girls. What would happen if he could not even get good grades?

After taking a chemistry midterm for which he had studied all weekend, David was convinced that he had blown it. "Why did I even bother killing myself over it?" he thought. That evening he saw some classmates at a local mall. When they asked him to go for a drive with them, he welcomed the chance. When they ended up in a deserted park and lit up marijuana joints, he could not say no. Most of the kids already thought he was an outsider; he wanted to show them he was not.

"It's only pot," he told himself. "I'm probably the only kid in school who hasn't tried it." David coughed and sputtered as he tried to hold the smoke in his lungs. But as he got stoned, he could feel himself relax. At last the pressure was off. The chemistry test did not seem to matter anymore. He was able to stop worrying about getting into college or making it in premed.

For a year David used marijuana only with others, and only on weekends. He kept his grades high enough to get into a top college. But by high school graduation, he wondered why he had spent all his life with his nose in a book. "It's time to have some fun!" he thought. For him, fun meant getting high.

David's parents noticed that he was becoming irritable and alienated. "Just a phase," they told themselves. "He's finally acting like other kids." All through the summer David was high more often than not. "This is crazy," he would tell himself, but he could not make himself stop. "When I get to college, I'll quit," he pledged.

When he moved into his dorm room, David realized that he was totally on his own. No one was watching him, telling him what to do, or paying attention to when he got up, whether he went to class, or what time he got in at night. He felt liberated, as if he had finally become an adult.

Drugs were easy to get on campus. "I'll stay away from the hard stuff," David told himself. "No one ever gets into trouble just smoking pot." He began getting high every day. Without even thinking about it, David began to cut his afternoon classes. He would go back to his dorm, turn on the television, and light up a joint.

"I'll study in a few hours," he would say, but the hours drifted by and he never got around to opening his books. The grades on his midterms were shockingly low. His parents thought he was having a hard time adjusting to being away from home. David felt that he simply was not as smart as everyone had thought.

He did not think drugs were to blame. "I'm only doing pot," he told himself. "That can't be the problem." But after a few months, David started forgetting things. "Often I couldn't remember what day it was, what I'd done the night before. If someone interrupted me when I was talking, I'd forget what I was saying."

Emotionally David felt as if he were riding a roller coaster. "I'd feel depressed and angry and paranoid all at the same time. Sometimes I'd be at a party, dancing and having a great time. Then something would happen, like a switch being flipped, and I'd start crying. I began to think I was losing my mind."

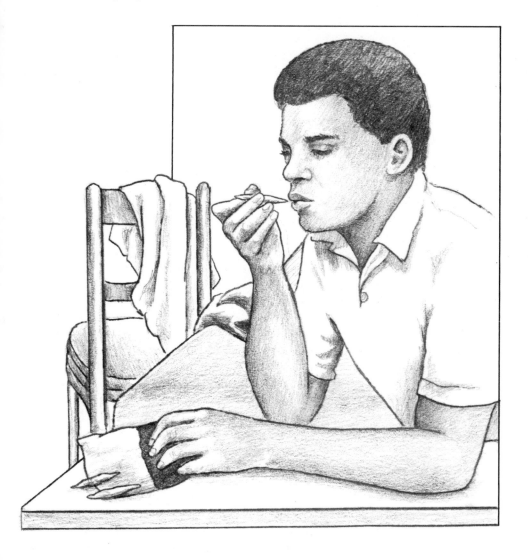

As the days turned colder and darker, David's spirits sank lower. More and more, he thought about killing himself — how and where he would do it, what he would say in his note. Then he would realize what he was thinking, and he would be terrified.

David describes the way he felt during the time he was using marijuana as "strained." He recalls, "Everything was a real strain. It hurt to breathe. My chest ached so much that it felt as if someone had tied a rope around me and was pulling it tighter and tighter. Once in a while I would feel this pressure, as if someone were standing on my chest and I couldn't breathe."

The emotional pain was just as great. "Mentally every little thing was a strain. It felt like my head was filled with air, that I couldn't make the connections to figure out how to do the simplest things." David stopped going to all his classes. He spent his days in a stupor.

When David went home for Thanksgiving, his parents were shocked. Their cleancut son had turned into a scruffy, bad-smelling stranger with behavior to match.

From the moment he got home, he deliberately taunted them. "They were the enemy," he explains. "I'd curse in front of them, using every four-letter word I knew, and I'd think, 'Boy, this is going to get them.' I stopped combing my hair or taking showers, just to see how they'd react. Before I'd never smoked a joint at home. Then I thought, 'What the hell?' I'd light up in my room and not even think about whether they'd smell the smoke."

When David's mother and father asked if he was using drugs, he denied it. Then, feeling an odd sense of relief, he poured out everything: his smoking, his moods, his fears of losing his sanity. They all cried.

"I want to be the way I was," he said, weeping. "I want everything to be the way it was." David dropped out of school for the rest of the semester and returned home to begin an outpatient rehabilitation program.

Looking back, David feels lucky that he had not experimented with other drugs. "Look at all the trouble I got into with pot," he says with a sad smile.

During rehabilitation David focused on sorting out his parents' expectations from his own interests and desires. "I finally realized that I didn't really want to become a doctor. That was what my folks thought I should do. I was just trying to please them."

His self-esteem bolstered by professional counselors, David sat down with his parents and talked about his past and the future. With their approval, he decided to start college all over again. He chose a school with a strong program in anthropology, a subject he had always loved.

"I thought my folks would be disappointed, but they weren't," he says. "I was so amazed to discover that they still loved me even after I'd screwed up at college. If I'd known that from the start, if I'd just believed in myself, maybe I never would have started smoking pot."

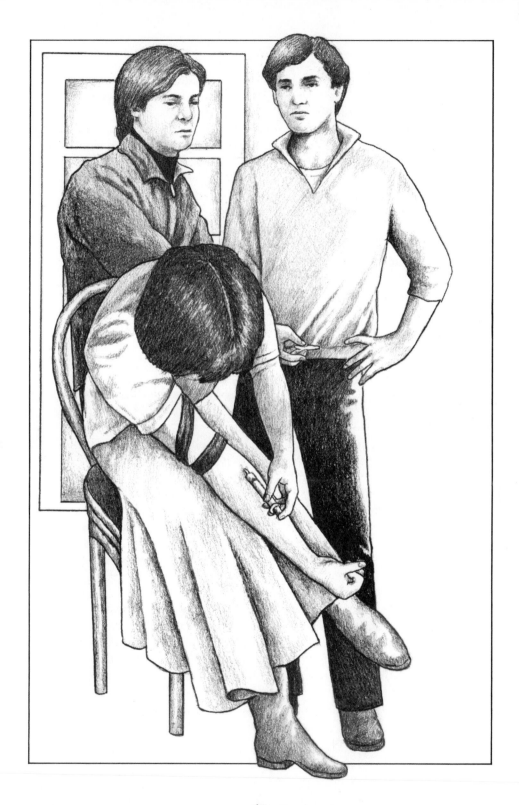

CHAPTER 4

SHERRI: FIFTEEN YEARS OF ADDICTION

Sherri Stewart's hands trembled as she formed a noose with her belt and hung it from a tall tree. "This is the only way," she told herself over and over as tears streamed down her face. "I've tried everything else. I've got to kill myself."

As Sherri pulled the belt taut, it snapped in two. Sobbing hysterically, she collapsed in the dirt. After 15 years of addiction, she knew that her body could not tolerate drugs any longer. But she also felt she could not live without them.

"How did I end up here?" she remembers thinking. "How did this happen to me?" No one could have answered her questions. Sherri had always been a golden girl. She grew up in an affluent suburb of Omaha, Nebraska. Her father was a well-known lawyer; her mother, a skilled homemaker and devoted wife. Her older brother had been a star athlete, a hero of the local high school. Sherri seemed to fit right into the picture: she was pretty, smart, popular, editor of the school newspaper, a cheerleader, and an honors student.

Yet always, deep inside, Sherri had the chilling feeling that she was a fake. Maybe she was good, but she was convinced she was not good enough. Sooner or later someone was sure to show the world that she really was not so special.

In high school, Sherri's friends started sneaking liquor to parties. She was 13 the first time she got drunk, and she liked the loose, giddy way it made her feel.

On a date with a college student when she was 15, Sherri — who had always looked and acted older than her age — smoked her first marijuana joint. Marijuana seemed far more daring and wicked than alcohol. She was not only intrigued by this new drug but also welcomed the release from tension it brought her. When she was high, she did not have to worry about whether she measured up to her "perfect" image.

Sherri began spending more time with kids who had a constant supply of drugs. After a few months of smoking marijuana she tried two hallucinogenic drugs — LSD and mescaline. Whereas marijuana calmed her down, the LSD and mescaline took her on electric trips, away from all her problems. She could run away without going anywhere.

Rather than waiting for friends to offer her drugs, Sherri started to buy her own. To earn money, she became a dealer, selling marijuana and LSD at school. Her suppliers operated out of bad neighborhoods far from her home, but she was willing to take any risks to get drugs. One day, while waiting in a dingy hallway to buy drugs, she spied through a half-open apartment door some young men who were injecting something into their arms. They saw her watching them. "Hey, honey, want to try some speed?" one of them called to her. She hesitated a moment. The idea of being stuck with a needle gave her the creeps, but she was nonetheless drawn to the dangerous scene. "Why not?" she thought.

Within seconds the powerful stimulant was coursing through her veins. She felt an intense, incredible rush. "Wow," she thought, "I'm traveling at warp speed now." As soon as the effect wore off she wanted to zoom up to those dizzying heights again.

Soon Sherri was starting and ending every day with a drug: marijuana before classes, LSD in home room, amphetamines at lunch. "I wanted to see how much I could get away with," she says. "I loved the challenge."

That was also the reason she kept going to school. "I wanted to show everyone that I could do drugs and still get good grades. I figured that if I kept my parents and teachers happy, they would never take my drugs away."

But Sherri's relationship with her parents began to crumble. She resented what she considered to be their constant interference in her personal life and began to argue with them almost daily. As Sherri's parents tried to set limits on her behavior, Sherri rebelled even more. She ran away from home and moved into a low-rent rooming house near her dealer. Over the next few weeks she took increasing amounts of amphetamines to stay high. Although she continued to attend school, Sherri was slipping into an amphetamine-induced state of emotional and physical derangement. She lost 30 pounds, began having memory blackouts, and was becoming more and more paranoid.

Sherri's frantic parents decided to have her arrested as a runaway. The police barged into one of her senior classes in the middle of a test and led her away. She thought they were taking her to jail. Instead, they took her to a hospital.

Alone in a cell-like room with steel bars, Sherri could not get the drugs she craved. She screamed at the nurses and threatened the attendants. Her parents had her admitted to a psychiatric hospital. But Sherri figured that if she told the staff what they wanted to hear, they would let her out.

"I guess I've just been hanging out with the wrong crowd," she said at the counseling sessions. Soon she had convinced her therapists that she was simply a confused young girl suffering the normal turmoil of adolescence.

When Sherri was released, she headed for the person who meant the most to her: her dealer. That night she smoked marijuana, took LSD, and swallowed pills. She hallucinated for a day, and suffered extreme depression when the effects wore off. Badly shaken, she went back to the hospital.

Although she wanted desperately to stay "straight," Sherri was haunted by her craving for drugs, convinced that she could not make it without them. Friends smuggled dope in to her at the hospital. While hospitalized — and taking drugs — she was given her senior final exams. Not only did she pass, she passed with flying colors.

In spite of her hospitalization, Sherri remained "hooked" on amphetamines. After her release, she began taking more and more of this drug, and her mental state deteriorated further. Because of her increasing paranoia, she would at times lock herself in her room with the curtains pulled, the door padlocked, and a shotgun — taken from her father's gun collection — in her lap. She bought a police radio and listened to it for hours, sure that the police were closing in on her.

But despite her drug abuse, despite the hospitalizations, associations with hard-core drug addicts, and patterns of disturbed behavior in general, there was another side to Sherri. Incredibly, on one level she was still functioning as a bright and successful student, making top grades and involving herself in a variety of extracurricular activities. As we have seen, she even managed to "ace" the senior finals she took while institutionalized for substance abuse.

On the basis of her outstanding academic record, and just as importantly, because of her ability to present herself well at the admissions interview, Sherri was accepted into a first-rate college. She made the dean's list in her junior and senior years and was accepted into a medical school.

"I can do anything," Sherri thought, "just as long as I have my drugs." In her medical school classes, she learned about prescription drugs; she began taking them regularly. Outside of classes she became adept at lying, sneaking, and stealing.

After graduation, Sherri chose psychiatry as her specialty and ended up as a resident psychiatrist in the same hospital where she had been hospitalized a few years before. The senior doctors considered her an outstanding young physician. The staff marveled at her insight and skill in working with addicts and alcoholics. But even as she cared for these troubled patients, she never thought of herself as one of them.

"I'm immune," she told

herself. "I'll never get so strung out. I'm in control." But soon Sherri started losing the control in which she took such great pride. Her world, so dependent on drugs, began to crumble.

She bickered with her coworkers and was almost constantly sick or in pain. She grew increasingly depressed.

In addition, soon Sherri reached a state in which she could not get high anymore. At an earlier stage she had become euphoric by injecting huge doses of narcotics into her veins. Now she was not responding at all. Marijuana and amphetamines just made her feel normal, and by this time, feeling "normal" was not feeling very well at all.

In the last stages of her addiction, Sherri was using twelve different drugs daily in quantities so enormous that she could not get enough from four different suppliers. Sometimes she would inject a gram of pure cocaine — a potentially lethal dose — into her veins. And as a doctor, she realized that she had pushed her mind and her body to the brink.

Finally two of her physician colleagues confronted Sherri and insisted that she get help. If she did not, she would lose the one thing in her life that she still valued: her medical license. Sherri bought a one-way ticket to a special rehabilitation program for physicians.

"If they can't cure me, I'll kill myself," she decided. After 36 hours without drugs, that was exactly what she tried to do. Some attendants found her sobbing and clutching the belt with which she had hoped to hang herself.

"I'm crazy, right?" Sherri asked.

"Yes," they said. "But only because you've been abusing drugs for so long." All her symptoms, they assured her, were caused by withdrawal, not mental illness.

Sherri's detoxification took a long time. She had abused drugs for as long as a person could without death ensuing. Her body and mind were literally "wasted." As the drugs slowly began to leave her system, she grew angry and fearful.

Unable to control herself, she lashed out at everyone around her. If there was a rule, she broke it. If there was a restriction, she tried to find a way around it.

Sherri clung to one simple idea: if she did not use drugs, she would survive. But she was sure she would never lose

her uncontrollable desire for drugs. After months of treatment, still deeply depressed, she walked to the bank of a nearby river. Staring out at the gray water, she started to cry. Then she sank to her knees and began to pray.

"Help me," she whispered despairingly. "I can't do it alone." She stayed on the ground for a long, long time. When she stood up, she felt as if a huge burden had been lifted from her shoulders. The compulsion to use drugs was gone. It never returned.

After completing her treatment, Sherri realized what she wanted to do with the rest of her life: help young people with drug problems. She joined the staff of the hospital where she had found help, and now specializes in treating adolescents with problems similar to her own.

Sherri has married, settled into a comfortable life, and found what she describes as "a freedom I'd never imagined possible." To this day, she does not understand why she became an addict. She is simply thankful that she made it through her fifteen years of addiction and that she no longer has to live in a chemical hell.

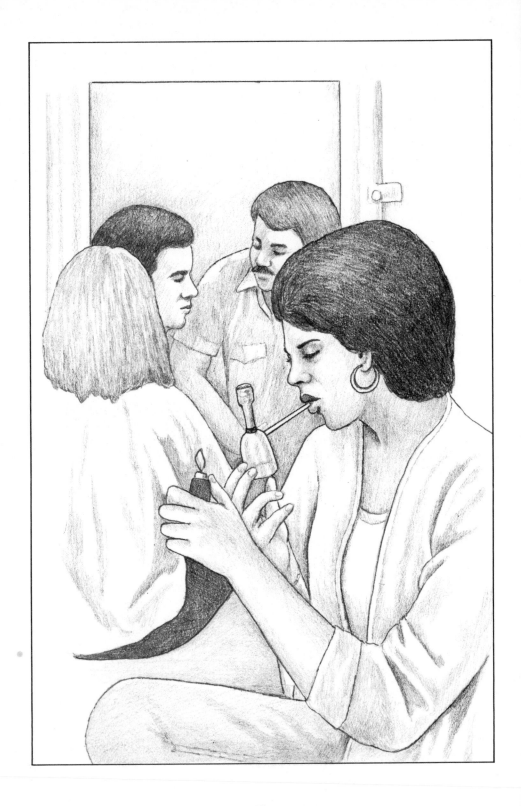

CHAPTER 5

BONNIE:
MOTHER AND CHILD

Bonnie Jones does not know why she ever allowed herself to have that first drug experience. She was 15, petite, and pretty. She had lots of friends in her Atlanta high school. She loved her parents and felt good about her life. She had never been interested in drugs. If she went to a party where kids were smoking marijuana, Bonnie would shake her head "no." She had had a few beers, but did not like the way it made her feel.

But one night her friends had something new: crack.

Bonnie knew they were talking about a form of cocaine that was broken down into pellets and smoked through a glass pipe. She could not imagine shooting drugs into her veins or snorting them into her nose. But suddenly, a simple smoke did not seem to be such a big deal. No one made much of a fuss over marijuana; why should they say anything about smoking crack, which could not be that much different?

But it was. Bonnie had heard about the "rush" of crack, a sensation some people had described as the ultimate high. She certainly had never experienced anything like it. She got so high that she felt she would never stop soaring. But in a few minutes she fell back into reality. The first thing she said was, "Give me more."

Bonnie kept smoking crack all that evening. The next day, a Saturday, she was exhausted and slept until noon. That night she went out looking for kids who might have some crack. But soon Bonnie wanted more crack than her friends were willing to give her for free. When they demanded money, she started withdrawing cash from her college savings fund. She sold her tape deck, her 10-speed bike, the pearls her grandmother had left her as a final gift.

As she became a daily user, Bonnie began to change inside and out. She lost so much weight that the outline of her ribs was visible under her sweater. This weight loss was not surprising, since cocaine is well known as an appetite suppressant. She started skipping classes. She would bleach her hair white one night and spray it pink the next. She coughed all the time.

Bonnie's craving for crack kept growing. One weekend, following a friend's whispered directions, she made her way to a seedy rooming house in a neighborhood she had never been in before.

In the hallway of the house she found a line of people. Just looking at them scared her, but nothing could make her leave. When her turn came, she slipped money — stolen from her mother's purse — through a slot in the door. Out came a packet of crack.

Bonnie became a regular. If she did not have money, she would start talking with some of the men in line. Most of them were friendly, and they would share some of their crack without asking for anything in return. Then one night a man insisted on sex as part of the bargain.

At first Bonnie said no. A few hours later, desperate to get high, she finally agreed. Afterward she felt completely disgusted with herself. But as soon as she got high again, it did not seem to matter anymore. She decided not to think about it.

Alarmed at their lovely daughter's transformation into a tough-talking, streetwise girl over the course of a few months, Bonnie's parents told her that if she did not change her behavior she would be confined to the house and only be allowed to have friends over for short visits on weekends.

Convinced that they would never carry through on their threats, Bonnie kept breaking their rules. She would stay out for nights at a time, returning home only when she needed a place to sleep. When her parents tried to talk to her, she would puff on a cigarette and blow smoke in their faces. "Why don't you just chill out and leave me be?" she would say.

Bonnie stopped going to school. Days and nights began to blur together. In the chaos of her drugged existence, Bonnie could not remember whether or not she had eaten or whom she had been with the night before.

By the time she realized she was pregnant, she was in her sixth month, too late for a safe abortion. Bonnie panicked. She had been using crack heavily throughout her pregnancy. She had no idea who the baby's father was. And she had nowhere to turn for help.

A friend loaned her money to see a doctor. She spent it on crack. One night, coming off a high, she felt a stabbing pain in her abdomen. "It can't be the baby," she thought. "It's way too soon."

Her son — a boy she named Jason — was born almost eight weeks premature, in the city hospital's emergency room. Labor was short and hard, and Bonnie, crashing and screaming, could not remember much about the delivery.

Jason was born a cocaine addict. The first three weeks of his life, he suffered the agonies of withdrawal. Since he had also been born too soon and too small, his hold on life was precarious. No one could predict whether he would live or whether he would suffer permanent damage.

Hooked up to monitors and tubes, Jason looked no bigger than a doll. His arms and legs were matchstick-slim; his skin looked as dry and thin as tissue paper. He could not breathe on his own. His heart stopped beating several times. His movements were jerky and uncoordinated. His vision was severely impaired.

Bonnie spent hours in the intensive care nursery every day, watching her tiny son fight for life in his incubator. "Crack did this to him," she thought, and wept. "I've done this to him. It's all my fault."

Bonnie's parents promised they would help her support and care for Jason — but only if she agreed to enter a drug treatment center. Bonnie made a pact with God: if God would save her son, she would give up drugs forever. Keeping her part of the deal was far from easy.

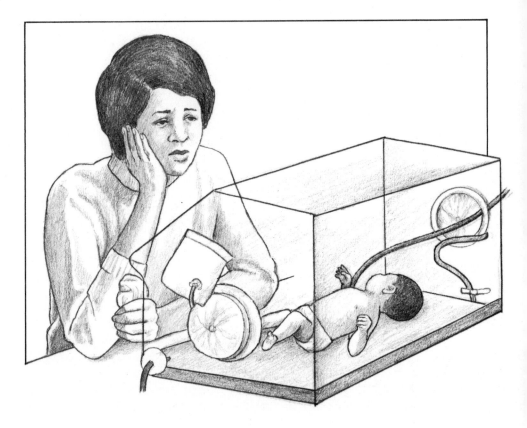

During a painful two-week withdrawal period at a treatment center, Bonnie plummeted into a deep, vicious depression. She was paranoid and irritable and often hallucinated. "I've messed up everything," she would say over and over again. "I just about killed my own baby."

As the chemicals slowly left her body, Bonnie began to feel hope again. What she remembers most is that, after months of seeing the world in blacks and grays, she was able to notice colors once more.

Bonnie spent six months behind locked doors in the treatment center, cut off from the people, places, and substances that had gotten her into trouble. Her reward for good behavior was being allowed to see Jason, who was still in the intensive care nursery struggling for a chance at life.

Bonnie began attending school part-time — a new school, where she could get a fresh start. She was always accompanied by a former user who had been at the drug treatment center longer. After a semester, she became the "strong" one, helping a more recently recovered addict slowly reenter the normal world.

When Bonnie returned home, she attended meetings of Narcotics Anonymous every night. "I need that kind of on-going support," she says. "I want to stay off drugs, but with crack, you're never sure you're going to be strong enough to say no. Part of me remembers what it felt like to be high. But I'm not willing to pay the price again. Feeling good for a few minutes just isn't worth it."

Bonnie tries to take each day as it comes. At times, she looks at the other kids in her high school, so full of hope for the future, and wishes she could be like them again. "I don't feel young anymore," she says. "Too much has happened. But at least I have Jason."

At 14 months, Jason is about the size of an infant half his age. He still has not begun to sit or crawl. Most days he lies listlessly in his crib, his eyes rolling about, unable to focus on anything for more than a second. Bonnie has begun to take him to a special facility for disabled children.

"He's alive, and that's a miracle in itself," she says. "I'm going to do whatever I can, whatever I have to do to help him. He didn't ask to be born like this. I'm his mother. I want to make it up to him—if I can."

Getting Help

Drug addiction is a form of imprisonment. The drugs themselves are expensive and any pleasurable sensations of altered consciousness they induce are fleeting. Withdrawal can be painful, debilitating, and sometimes deadly. Many people who succumb to substance abuse are embroiled for years in the punishing web of dependency and tolerance, which involves constant cravings, ever-increasing doses, and repeated destructive assaults on the mind and body.

Once addiction takes hold, there is no guarantee that a permanent cure is possible. However, there are numerous treatment techniques and facilities available to help the addict make the long journey back to a drug-free existence. Experts differ on which of the many treatments for addiction is the most effective, but everyone seems to agree that the essential first step is a rock-solid commitment on the part of the addict to take control of his or her own life and avoid drugs absolutely.

Only a properly trained health-care professional can decide which treatment approach best suits any given individual. In the following photo essay, we highlight a few of the many rehabilitation facilities in operation throughout the United States. Being weaned from drug dependency takes time. Often, addicts are best served in a residential facility where all contact with the outside world is temporarily severed. Sometimes treatment involves vocational rehabilitation. Sometimes it involves individual and group therapy sessions. Usually, a combination of several different methods is required. In all cases, the user must undergo a reeducation of sorts, in which he or she learns that drug use is not a release from one's problems, but rather a crippling handicap.

As the case histories in this volume demonstrate, there is hope for the recovering addict. These photographs capture some of the small but memorable triumphs of people who have decided to come to terms with — and ultimately overcome —their illness.

Clara Hale holds one of her charges at Hale House, a home she founded in Harlem to treat withdrawal symptoms of infants born to addicted mothers.

Recovering addicts participate in a food distribution program for the poor at Synanon, a private rehabilitation center in California.

Patients at Phoenix House discuss the reasons people initially turn to drugs and learn about the harmful effects of these substances.

A former heroin addict at New York's Daytop Village learns to operate a pipe-threading machine. Patients who learn skills here are better equipped to reenter the job market when they leave the center.

In 1983 Dr. Mark S. Gold founded 800-COCAINE, a hotline that aids callers struggling with cocaine addiction. The 24-hour service is available to users seeking immediate help and can advise them where to go to begin long-term therapy.

A patient at New York's Horizon House does some house painting. This sort of activity is often therapeutic for recovering addicts.

A moment of reflection for a patient six weeks into his treatment at New York City's Odyssey House.

Recovering addicts at Phoenix House meet with Nancy Reagan, who is at the forefront of the national campaign against drug abuse. At right is Dr. Mitchell Rosenthal, president of Phoenix House.

A former drug addict leaves a rehabilitation center prepared to meet the challenge of a life without drugs—a challenge that he must face and conquer every day for the rest of his life.

CHAPTER 6

NICK:
A COKEAHOLIC'S TALE

By the time he was 30, Nick Bartucci was making more than $250,000 a year as a stockbroker in Chicago. He drove an expensive car, wore custom-made suits, and lived in a penthouse condominium with a magnificent view of Lake Michigan.

Nick's success delighted him. He would smile when he thought about making more money than his big brother, Adam. After all, Adam was the one who earned all the As and won all the awards in school. Yet here Nick was — the "slow" one—with a net worth climbing toward $1 million.

However, Nick's success sometimes left him with a hollow, lonely feeling. He had few close friends, and although he dated, he found it difficult to have a long-term relationship with a woman.

When his spirits slumped, Nick had a way of picking them up: cocaine. Within minutes of snorting a few lines, he would feel invincible, certain that he could take on the world and win. With cocaine, he did not need anyone else.

But Nick had always been wary of drug addiction, so he limited his use. "I know what I'm doing," he told himself. "I know how to use it without getting hooked." Then, one night at a party, Nick *freebased* (smoked a heated mixture of co-caine and ether) for the first time.

As he inhaled, his heart raced and his breathing quick-ened. He felt as if he were Clark Kent turning into Superman. Everyone in the room seemed to fade away. Within ten min-utes, Nick wanted more cocaine.

He continued to freebase throughout the party. Never before had he felt such a craving. At the end of the night he asked the host for the name of his dealer.

Nick tried to limit his freebasing, to restrict himself as he had before. But even when he was at his office, caught up in an important transaction, he would find himself thinking about freebasing. The craving would grow and grow until he could not control it anymore.

Nick began freebasing more often. On a Friday night he'd buy several hundred dollars' worth of cocaine and invite a woman to spend the weekend with him. Sometimes he and his date would not sleep from Friday through Sunday. The weekends turned into one long high.

Mondays were hell. As the effects of the drug wore off, he could not believe how bad he felt — worse than he had imagined was even possible. He could not stop shaking, could not keep any food down, could not focus his racing mind on anything.

Swigging liquor and gulping down tranquilizers to dull the pain, Nick forced himself to go back to work. But all he could think about was cocaine. He began freebasing daily. In three months he spent $50,000 on the drug.

"What's wrong with Nick?" his coworkers would ask. Previously athletic and well-built, he stopped jogging and eating regularly. He lost 60 pounds and looked emaciated. When he started making crucial mistakes in business trans-actions, his clients deserted him for more reliable brokers.

Worried, his brother badgered him about seeing a doc-tor. His colleagues, beginning to suspect a drug problem, also urged him to get help. But the only aid Nick sought was financial; he borrowed money from everyone he knew. He sold his fancy car and put his condominium on the market. He needed every dollar he could get for cocaine.

Nick no longer felt any rush of pleasure when he free-based. All he wanted, all he got, was an end to the depression

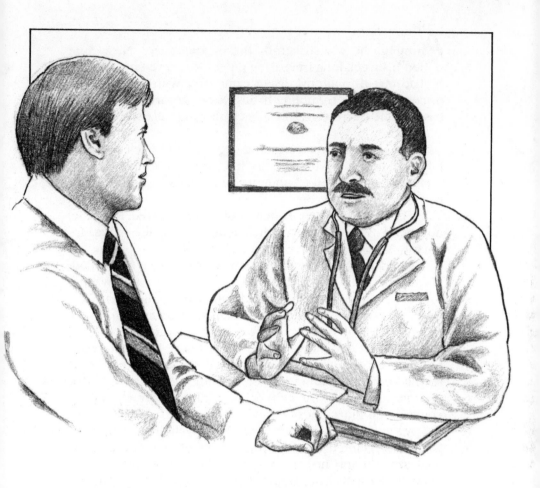

he felt when he was not on drugs. Yet when he freebased, he would often feel his heart pounding so wildly that he feared it would leap out of his chest. Frightened, he finally consulted a doctor, who warned him that his heartbeat was irregular.

"It could be serious," the doctor said. "Be careful." Nick did not dare ask about the danger of freebasing. "I'll quit," he promised himself. "I can do it."

But he could not. Instead his addiction grew. The drugs began to make him paranoid; he became certain that people were following him in the streets, trying to steal his drugs or report him to the police. Sometimes he would hallucinate that the phone was ringing or voices were shouting at him.

Although he was shaken by these experiences, Nick continued his week-long freebasing binges. One evening a friend he had met through his dealer came over with a new batch of cocaine. With trembling hands, Nick prepared it for freebasing. The two men sat in silence, passing a glass pipe back and forth.

The cocaine seemed incredibly strong to Nick, and the jolt he felt seemed to electrify his heart. He looked across the room at his friend. Suddenly he realized that something had gone terribly wrong.

The man's eyes were open. His lips were parted. He made no sound. When Nick touched him, he did not move. In horror, Nick realized that his friend was dead.

Panicked, Nick groped his way to the phone and called his brother. He sat on the couch, clutching a pillow and sobbing, until Adam arrived and called the police. As Nick came down from his high, he began to scream and thrash around. The police took him to a local emergency room.

The next day, at his brother's insistence, Nick entered a hospital. He thought he was dying. Every cell in his body seemed to be screaming. The craving for cocaine was almost unbearable. Finally, the cold reality hit him: there would be, could be no more cocaine—not ever again.

After the physical crash came a psychological plunge. Nick was haunted by the image of his dead friend and by guilt over the way he had wrecked his career. His money was gone, along with his job, his reputation, his health, and his beloved possessions. The road back seemed impossibly long.

But Nick took the first step. He started to participate in a therapy program as soon as he left the hospital. Slowly rebuilding his self-confidence, he found a new job. In the beginning, almost any problem would make him think about cocaine, but he would call his therapist instead of buying drugs. One day at a time, he managed to cope.

The hardest part was learning, for the first time in his life, how to reach out and relate to other people — particularly to women. For a while Nick did not even want to date. But in his new office he met an attractive woman who became his friend, and then his wife.

Nick no longer lives in the fast lane. He and Sally have a modest ranch-style house in a suburb west of Chicago. They spend their weekends bicycling, cross-country skiing, or watching movies on their VCR. "This is the good life," says Nick. "When I look back, I think of how lucky I've been. I fell in love with cocaine, and it nearly killed me. I'm just thankful that it didn't."

CHAPTER 7

SANDY: NO PLACE TO RUN

Sandy Hanson belonged to a large family. She was much younger than her brothers and sisters and never felt she received much attention from them or her parents. As a child Sandy would create elaborate daydreams as a means of escape. Several times she packed a suitcase and announced that she was running away, but she always returned to her amused parents after going only a few blocks down the road.

As she grew up, Sandy decided that she was not getting attention because she had not done anything to earn it. She decided to work extra hard at school — maybe if she did well enough, her family would notice her.

This need to do well academically eventually became an obsession. There never seemed to be enough hours in the day to study. At times, Sandy thought about how much more she could achieve if she did not have to sleep — if only she could work 24 hours a day.

When Sandy was 14, a classmate gave her an amphetamine. Sandy swallowed the pill and within half an hour felt a surge of power and strength, as if she could leap over the highest building. "I've got a wonderful new friend," she thought. She believed she had finally found something that would help her impress her family.

71

RECORDS & TAPES

Getting the drugs was no real problem. She was able to obtain some "uppers" from friends. Then, although she was not seriously overweight, she went to several doctors in a nearby city who prescribed amphetamines for "appetite control." Armed with these prescriptions, she took them to a few "cooperative" pharmacists one of her friends had told her about. These druggists filled the prescriptions — and continued to fill them again and again, long after they had expired.

Sandy used amphetamines as fuel to propel her from one dazzling achievement to another. She believed that the drug enhanced her powers of concentration, sharpened her thinking, and lent incisiveness — even brilliance — to her term papers and essays. They also allowed her to function on very little sleep, increasing the time she could devote to her studies. She graduated from high school at the top of her class, and four years later earned a bachelor's degree — with honors — from an excellent university. Her teachers applauded her. Her parents praised her. Her brothers and sisters congratulated her. She entered graduate school.

Sandy had achieved her goal, but she could not enjoy the attention she was finally getting. She feared that if her family ever found out the truth, they would reject her. They were religious and conservative. She could not imagine what they would think about her drug use.

Of course, Sandy always felt she was different from other drug users. After all, she didn't take drugs because she liked them; she took them because she had to. She had tried "party drugs," such as pot, cocaine, and LSD, but she rarely used drugs just to have a good time. To her, speed was not a recreational drug; it was something different and absolutely essential. She did not know how to function without it.

But it had reached the point where she wasn't functioning well with it, either. Sometimes she would not sleep for a week at a time, and would become so irrational that she could not carry on a conversation. She hallucinated that she was hearing voices and seeing bizarre creatures. She would snap at anyone who spoke to her. Sometimes she would reach a state in which she could not get any higher, regardless of how much speed she took.

At these times she became suspicious of everyone around her. She withdrew, isolating herself from her family and friends. Although her body ached for sleep, her mind could not rest. When she could get them, she would take barbiturates (sedatives) to get to sleep, but they usually made her so sick that she would vomit.

Sandy had always told herself that she took drugs only when she needed them. But lately that meant all the time. She had a minor car accident and "needed" something. She quarreled with her parents and "needed" something. She was on the verge of flunking out of graduate school and "needed" something.

By this time, Sandy's life revolved around pills. She would buy as many as she could — on the street, from unscrupulous doctors and pharmacists, from friends and dealers — and hoard them in her room. When visiting her friends she would steal pills from their medicine cabinets, looking them up in the *Physicians' Desk Reference* to see what diseases they were meant to treat. She would then convince herself that she had the exact symptoms each medication was designed to relieve.

Sandy dropped out of graduate school, saying she had had enough of teachers and classes. She got a job, but soon lost it. She tried running away again—literally.

Sandy hopscotched from city to city, always blaming different places, jobs, and people when things did not work out. Constantly "wired," she thought drugs were helping her cope with the chaos of her life. In reality they were responsible for it. When she ran out of money for drugs, Sandy shoplifted. Once she was caught and arrested, but she was released because it was her first offense.

A couple of times she overdosed, waking up in a hospital emergency room feeling as if every cell in her body were about to explode. She began to sink into depression and to think about killing herself.

Terrified of what speed was doing to her, she swore never to use it again. She foolishly thought that if she switched to "organic" drugs, like marijuana and alcohol, rather than pills, she could achieve the "highs" she so desperately craved, without doing such violence to her health.

Sandy got a new job in a new city. But without even realizing what she was doing, she began dangerously to abuse alcohol and food. If she was not drinking, she was eating. Her weight ballooned. Horrified by her appearance, she took speed to control her appetite. Soon she was using more than ever. And she was scared.

Finally one day Sandy looked at her drawn face and bloodshot eyes in a mirror and decided to get help. She was so exhausted and upset when she went to her first Narcotics Anonymous meeting that she cannot remember what anyone said to her, but the feeling of love and acceptance was so strong that she went back.

As she kept going to meetings, she stopped using amphetamines although she continued to drink heavily and to smoke marijuana. One evening she admitted her continuing drug use to the group. To her surprise, no one criticized her. Many of them had done the same at some time, but they tried to convince her that she could not recover unless she abstained from all drugs.

"Marijuana and alcohol are not drugs," she insisted. "They're like tobacco." No one argued. The group members just shook their heads and encouraged her to keep coming to the meetings.

Sandy did. Month after month, she sat and listened to the stories of other addicts. She knew that once they had felt the same way that she did about drugs. Yet they had found ways to live without them. "Can I do it, too?" she wondered.

Sandy kept telling the group that she did not want to give up drugs entirely. But deep down she knew that she really was afraid she would fail. With the group's encouragement, Sandy sought help from a drug counselor. "Maybe I can do it," she said, daring to hope that she could.

Sandy was making some progress in the struggle to overcome her addictions but suffered a severe setback during the Christmas holidays. Long estranged from her family, she did not get any gifts. A man that she had started dating broke off their relationship. She learned of the suicide of an old friend. Once more Sandy began to use speed, aggravating this problem with alcohol. She woke up on a cold rainy New Year's Day, feeling desperately alone.

Then the phone rang. It was one of the members of Narcotics Anonymous, asking about her. Guiltily, she admitted that she had been doing a lot of drugs. Her new friend was concerned — not angry, not judgmental, but genuinely worried about her. "No one else ever even cared," she says.

That evening at the group meeting, Sandy promised that she would not use drugs again before calling one of the members. To this day, she has not had to make that call. She has also been able to stop running away from her problems and herself. "I kept thinking that there was some magic place where I could find all the attention I ever needed," she says. "I thought all I had to do was look hard enough. Now I've realized that you don't find places like that — you make them yourself."

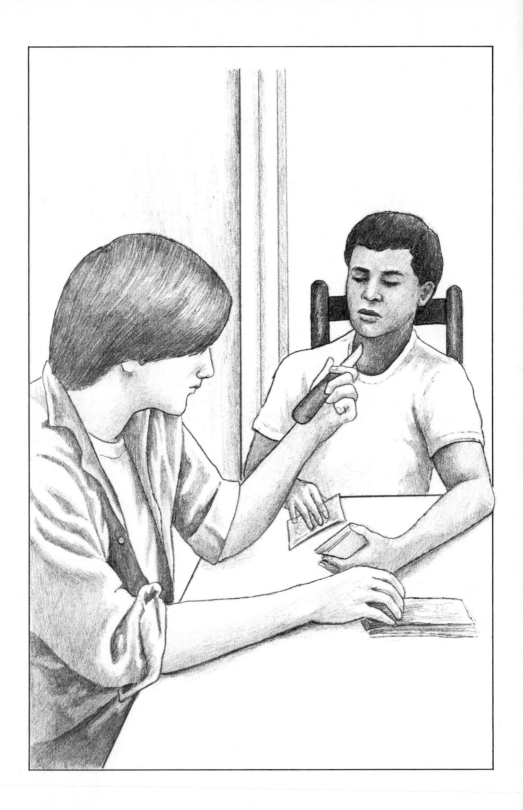

CHAPTER 8

JEFF: LIFE AND DEATH ON THE STREETS

The scene was an urban nightmare, a street of peepshows and pornographic bookstores and bars that never closed. Prostitutes of all ages and both sexes stood in the doorways. Drug dealers wove their way through the crowds, trading tiny packages for large amounts of money.

To 18-year-old Jeff, this place had been home for much of the last four years. When he ran away to Los Angeles from the small town in Indiana where he had grown up, he had nowhere to turn. He did not have much to leave behind: his mother was an alcoholic, his father had deserted them long ago, and he had experienced many run-ins with the law. He had always been a street kid, the type that people said would end up in trouble.

Jeff quickly learned to do whatever he had to do to survive on the streets. Drugs were everywhere, and they quickly became part of his life. He became a "runner," delivering drugs for the street's big dealers to their clients across town. He was fast and reliable, and he asked for his increasingly lavish tips in drugs.

As he got older, Jeff started dealing himself. First he sold PCP (a hallucinogenic drug) in movie theaters and on the street. As he made more money, he added LSD and cocaine to his inventory.

Jeff considered himself a smart businessman. When crack — or "rock," as they call it on the West Coast — hit the streets, he realized it could make him rich. This potent form of cocaine could be sold in "pellets" for $5 or $10. He could buy

pure cocaine, break it down into crack, and sell enough to become a big man on the street — someone everyone would want to know.

Jeff and a friend he knew from his days as a runner rented a rundown apartment above a bar. The place reeked of vomit and urine. Trash was piled in the hallways; graffiti covered the walls. None of that mattered to them.

In the kitchen Jeff and his partner mixed cocaine, baking soda, and water, heated it in a pot, and put the dried pieces into plastic bags. Jeff took half the drugs to a busy street corner. Kids from the suburbs, driving their parents' cars, would pull over to the curb to "stop and cop" (buy some crack). Within a few hours Jeff had made more money than he had ever had in his life.

Soon Jeff was running a full-fledged crack house. But the more Jeff sold, the more he used. At first if he smoked enough, he could stay high, feeling stimulated and excited for hours. But the crashes, the dreaded lurches into depression and sadness, got worse.

After a few weeks Jeff started feeling edgy all the time. He could not sleep. He began to suspect that people were closing in on him and bought a gun to keep in the apartment in case of a raid.

Jeff realized that he could not go on the way he had, and began to nurture a fantasy: he would put aside money every week, and when he had enough he would leave the streets and start over again.

Jeff figured out a way to get the money he needed to make his dream come true. For the last few months, he had been selling his customers high-quality crack, and they were hooked. He began to cut back on the amount of cocaine in the mixture. Sometimes he would use chunks of roasted peanuts or fine white powders — anything that was cheap and looked like crack.

To make sure his customers would get an unforgettable high, Jeff began lacing his packets with PCP. He knew what PCP could do, how it could trigger hallucinations of horrifying intensity. But he could not resist trying "space-basing" —combining cocaine and PCP—himself.

He had never had such a frightening experience. "I looked into the face of the devil," Jeff told his partner afterward. "And he knew my name."

Nevertheless, Jeff continued space-basing. He began to exhibit all the symptoms of paranoia and psychosis. He would hear voices where there were none. He became convinced that he was being followed. He had nightmares about bugs crawling all over him that were so vivid that he would awaken during the night with blood beneath his fingernails from clawing at his skin.

By day, his behavior became increasingly bizarre. Once he put his hand through a window; another time he held a knife under his partner's chin as he counted out their equal shares of the daily "take."

"You're out of control," his partner said before walking out. "You've got to get help."

Jeff did try to quit, but without drugs he could barely move. He plummeted into the blackness of a deep depression. Shaking, sweating, moaning, vomiting, Jeff felt that he would rather not live if he had to live without drugs. Soon he was space-basing again.

The night the police raided his apartment they were expecting a routine crack arrest. They pounded on the door. Inside they could hear the sounds of someone scurrying around.

By the time they broke down the door, the apartment looked empty, but the bathroom was locked. "Probably flushing the stuff down the john," said one of the officers.

Then they heard the blast. They found Jeff lying on the filthy floor of the bathroom, the gun still pointed at what was left of his face.

CHAPTER 9

MARIANNE: POOR LITTLE FAT GIRL

Chubby cheeks!" were the words scrawled under Marianne Bryant's first baby picture. But everyone thought the round-faced infant was adorable. It was not until later, when she started school, that the coos turned into cruel taunts.

"Pudge" was what her friends called her. "Fatso" was the name the other kids used. Even Marianne's father, a New Jersey factory worker who was heavy himself, teased her about her "baby fat."

"In our family, food was a reward," Marianne recalls. "If I got good grades, I'd get an extra slice of cake. If I helped around the house, I'd get ice cream. As I got older, I'd eat whenever I felt happy or depressed or bored. I had a thirty-six-inch waistline by the time I turned twelve."

In high school, Marianne was the fat girl no one dated. "The boys would make jokes about me. They'd say I was a human tub. I was so lonely and miserable that I found myself eating more and more. I hated my body, and I hated myself."

When she went to college, Marianne was determined to lose weight. She tried diet after diet. After starving herself for a few weeks, she would lose ten pounds. But inevitably she would regain the weight she lost—plus a little more.

Finally she tried something new. Every time she went on a binge and ate a lot of ice cream or pizza, she would go to the bathroom and force herself to throw up.

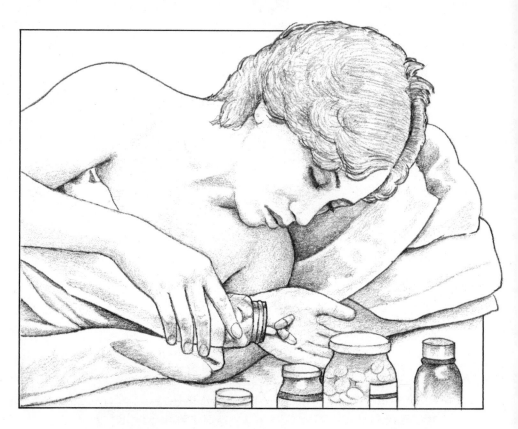

One of her roommates gave Marianne some diet pills. The pounds started to come off, but she felt so revved up by the stimulants in the pills that she could not get to sleep. Another friend suggested Valium, a tranquilizer. She began taking the stimulating diet pills during the day and Valium in the evening to help her sleep. She continued using these drugs even after she had slimmed down, and also continued binging and vomiting — symptoms characteristic of an eating disorder called bulimia.

Marianne did not have a serious romance until she was 22. At a singles bar, she met a smooth-talking man who made her feel beautiful. Soon she was head-over-heels in love.

One night her boyfriend told her he had brought a very special present: a gram of cocaine. Although she had abused pills for years, Marianne was scared of illegal drugs.

"But Mark uses it, and I love him, and he loves me," she told herself. "He's not going to give me anything that will hurt me."

Cocaine took Marianne out of the body she had loathed for so long. "For the first time in my life, I felt incredibly sexy," she recalls. Marianne discovered something else about cocaine: it made her forget about food. She would go for days without eating, and she lost weight rapidly.

Although she disliked the low that followed every high, Marianne continued to use cocaine. When her boyfriend's supply ran out, she would approach other men in bars, offering to buy cocaine for both of them. Once they gave her money, she would leave and never return.

One night, after taking Valium to help her come down from her high, she passed out at her boyfriend's apartment. When she woke up, he screamed at her, "You're no better than a junkie! Get out and stay out!"

She went home and gathered up all the pills she had stockpiled over the years — literally hundreds of them. Washing them down with straight vodka, she kept swallowing until she passed out. A neighbor found her the next morning and called an ambulance. The paramedics could not find any pulse. But a sensitive monitor finally picked up a faint heartbeat, and a team of doctors at the hospital was able to resuscitate her.

Embarrassed and frightened, Marianne swore she would never do drugs again. But even though she tried, she could not stay clean on her own. She started passing bad checks to get money for cocaine. Within a few weeks she was caught and imprisoned.

Marianne was too ashamed to call her family for money for bail, so she ended up spending two weeks behind bars.

"Nice girls don't end up in jail," she recalls thinking. "I couldn't believe it was happening to me. The most humiliating thing was that one of the kids in my high-school class was working there. When he realized who I was, he was shocked. I'll never forget the look on his face when he asked how I'd let this happen to me. I didn't know what to tell him. I didn't know myself."

The judge gave Marianne two choices: a prison term or drug rehabilitation. "I swore I'd do anything to get out of jail. Rehab sounded like a sweet deal. I figured I'd just listen and go along and be a good girl."

It was not that easy. In group therapy sessions, Marianne was forced to dig deep and confront feelings she had been burying all her life. "I had to come to terms with the little fat girl inside me, to learn how to give her the love she needed. It was the hardest thing I've ever done."

It was hard for her to focus only on herself, on her needs, desires, and abilities, rather than on what she could take to feel better. Marianne came to realize that all her life she had been turning to things — food, pills, cocaine — to make her feel right about herself.

"They were my props, something I could lean on because I didn't feel strong enough to face the world on my own," she says. Yet the people in the treatment program accepted her, even loved her, just as she was—without any "props."

Marianne also learned a great deal about food and eating. "I had to teach myself how to recognize when I was genuinely hungry and how to eat like a normal person," she says. "I'd never felt that I could control my weight on my own, but the counselors taught me how."

After two months in the program Marianne had a visitor: her old boyfriend. He wanted her back. She asked him if he was still using cocaine. "Yes, but I know how to handle it," he said. "I'll help you so next time you can handle it, too."

But Marianne knew there would not be, could not be, a next time. She knew she could not be around drugs without using them and could not use them without abusing them. For a long time she just sat still, looking at the man who had been the first to tell her she was pretty and to make her feel special. However, she knew he was the wrong man for her. She touched his cheek gently, got up, and walked out of the room.

"I wasn't strong enough to do that a year ago, even a month ago," she says. "I can't be sure I'd be strong enough to do it again tomorrow. When I said good-bye to him, I said good-bye to a lot of things — to drugs, to depending on someone or something else to tell me how to live, to the fat kid who'd do anything to be liked."

After leaving treatment Marianne got an apartment with another former cocaine addict. They gave each other support through some depressing times.

Marianne found that by talking about her feelings, she could defuse her desperate desire for something to make her feel better. She stopped binging on food and began exercising.

At 27, she looks and feels better than she ever has. "I'm not hiding behind fat or food or drugs anymore," she says. "I can face the world without leaning on anyone or anything."

CHAPTER 10

KEITH: A JUNKIE'S JOURNEY

In jail, Keith Phillips had a lot of time to look back and think about how he had ended up there. It seemed as if he had been in trouble all his life. The first time it happened he was just 11 years old.

He and Greg, a boy considered the wildest kid in their working-class neighborhood in Pittsburgh, became buddies. Their favorite game was building fires, competing against each other to make the biggest blaze. Once they accidentally burned a garage.

A couple of months later Keith and Greg broke into a house, found a wallet with $300 in it, and stole the money. A woman across the street spotted them. They had to return the money, but the neighbor agreed not to tell the police.

Keith liked the danger of these adventures. By comparison, school seemed boring. He never did homework or paid attention in class. His marks were just high enough to get him from one grade to the next. But when he entered junior high school, tests showed that he was a lot brighter than anyone had suspected. The school placed him in a special class with much more motivated students.

"For the first time, I was with kids who *liked* school. They always did their homework, always showed up for class, always wanted to learn new things. I became just like them. For a while, I was almost at the top of the class, and I stayed out of trouble on the streets."

When Keith and his mother moved to Philadelphia, he found himself in a different school and with a different crowd. At 13, he discovered that his new friends were less interested in classwork than they were in one particular extracurricular activity: smoking marijuana.

Keith knew enough about drugs to be wary of them, but he thought that he would not get into trouble if he stuck to marijuana. "I felt I had to go along so people wouldn't look down on me," he explains. "I was the new kid on the block."

In his letters to his old friends, Keith bragged about getting high every day. "Don't do it," they wrote back. "You're too smart for that." Keith knew he was smart — smart enough, he assumed, to do drugs without losing control.

As he smoked more and more pot, Keith again lost interest in school, and his grades tumbled. When one of his new friends asked him if he wanted in on some "action," Keith said yes. He soon found out that the "action" meant burglarizing houses. Keith was nervous, but he went along. They stole a stereo and a VCR, sold them, and used the money for drugs.

Keith spent less and less time at home — for many reasons. His mother had remarried, and his stepfather was an alcoholic. "I hated going home, because he was always drunk. He'd yell at my mother and take swings at me. I started spending more time on the streets, even though the only things to do there were get in trouble and get high. I did a lot of both."

When he was 14, Keith was arrested for burglary. He spent several weeks at a detention center for youthful criminal offenders. But Keith was able to convince the administrators that he had learned his lesson, and they released him.

A few months later Keith was arrested again and sent to another detention home. It was far more rigid and confining than the first one. It seemed like a prison. "I hated being there, and I hated everyone who put me there. I thought, 'I'm not going to change just to satisfy you. There is nothing you can do to make me.'"

By the time he was 16, Keith was more than a bad boy or a troubled kid. He was a tough young man with a criminal record and a chip on his shoulder. He dropped out of school, spending his days in pool halls or on street corners. The fights with his stepfather intensified, and he moved out.

Keith got a job working nights in a factory, but often he became so tired that he almost fell asleep on his feet. One night a man on the assembly line offered him a pill. He swallowed it without asking what it was. In less than an hour, he felt full of energy.

Stimulants such as amphetamines became part of Keith's daily diet. He figured if one made him feel good, ten would make him feel terrific. But the drugs were not without their negative effects. In a few months, Keith lost 30 pounds. "I need something new," he told his dealer. "Something better."

The man offered him some heroin. Keith had sworn he would never try "junk." "I don't need that kind of trouble," he used to say. "I've got enough already." But he figured that one hit would not hurt. "It'll just get me through tonight," he told himself.

The heroin took him to places he'd never known existed. He had never felt so good. "I fell in love," he recalls. "I thought, 'This is how I want to feel for the rest of my life.' "

At first Keith tried to limit his heroin use, but he could not. Every day he seemed to need a little more to take him to that special place, far away from all his problems. But whenever he came back down to earth, he would develop more problems.

He was late for work so often that his boss fired him. To make money, he started dealing drugs. But instead of selling his merchandise, he would often use it himself. When he ran out of credit with his supplier, he was desperate. He heard about a way to make a lot of money quickly: flying to the Caribbean and smuggling a new supply of heroin back into the country for several dealers.

After only a few runs, Keith was arrested and imprisoned for possession of heroin. He spent 13 months in prison. The first months of his sentence he went through a painful period of withdrawal from heroin.

"Never again," he told himself. He looked back on his short life and realized how much of it he had wasted on drugs and crime. But when he got out, Keith could think of only one thing: heroin. His mother loaned him money to make a new start; he spent it all on drugs. In a few weeks, he was back on the streets, dealing and stealing. Then he overdosed.

"I came so close to dying that it seemed easier just to let go, to bring it all to an end," he recalls. "But part of me wouldn't let go. That's the part that realized I needed help." He agreed to work on his problems, and his probation officer referred him to a drug-treatment program.

At first Keith was not sure anyone could help him. "Once a junkie, always a junkie," he thought. For six months he could not stop thinking about getting high. The only thing that helped was sitting in group meetings, listening to addicts just like him tell their stories. These people once had needed drugs just as much as he did, yet somehow they had found a way to live without them. "Maybe I can, too," Keith said to himself.

In counseling sessions, Keith began to search for ways to put his shattered world back together. "I realized that all my life, I never cared about people. I didn't even care about myself, about my body. All I wanted was drugs. I wasn't in control. The drugs were. I was obsessed with money so I could get drugs. I didn't care about anything else."

With the therapists' help, Keith confronted his past. "I used to think I knew everything. But when I looked, really looked, at what I was, I was nothing. I was hanging around with people who were killing themselves, who were in and out of jail, who didn't care about their own lives, let alone mine. I asked myself, 'Do I want to spend the rest of my life like that? Do I want to let other people control me?' I had to admit I didn't know everything, and I never would."

As he learned more about drugs and their effects on the body, Keith came to a decision that surprised even him: "I didn't want any drugs in me. I didn't want to waste my life. I realized that since I can't control drugs, my only hope is to stay away from them altogether."

After leaving the rehabilitation center, Keith moved away from his drug-using friends. "'Friends' isn't the right word," he says. "They don't care about themselves, so how could they care about me?"

Keith also began to mend his relationships with his mother and stepfather. "My mom noticed a change in me right away. She and I sat down and talked, really talked, for hours. She talked me into moving back with them for a while. When my stepfather got help with his drinking problem, things really changed between us. I like to think it helped him to have me there. I knew what he was going through, because I'd been there, too."

Best of all, Keith met Erin, a fellow "graduate" of the rehabilitation program. Both understood how vulnerable they were to drugs. But together they felt they could make a new life — a life built not on chemicals, but on love, trust, and hope.

Keith took evening classes to earn his high-school diploma and went on to a local junior college. He and Erin were married. A few years later, they had a son.

"It's still hard for me to think about my past," says Keith. "I came so close to blowing my whole life. But I'm not going to blow the future—not for my sake, or Erin's, or my son's."

APPENDIX

State Agencies
for the Prevention and Treatment
of Drug Abuse

ALABAMA
Department of Mental Health
Division of Mental Illness and
    Substance Abuse Community
    Programs
200 Interstate Park Drive
P.O. Box 3710
Montgomery, AL 36193
(205) 271-9253

ALASKA
Department of Health and Social
    Services
Office of Alcoholism and Drug
    Abuse
Pouch H-05-F
Juneau, AK 99811
(907) 586-6201

ARIZONA
Department of Health Services
Division of Behavioral Health
    Services
Bureau of Community Services
Alcohol Abuse and Alcoholism
    Section
2500 East Van Buren
Phoenix, AZ 85008
(602) 255-1238

Department of Health Services
Division of Behavioral Health
    Services
Bureau of Community Services
Drug Abuse Section
2500 East Van Buren
Phoenix, AZ 85008
(602) 255-1240

ARKANSAS
Department of Human Services
Office of Alcohol and Drug Abuse
    Prevention
1515 West 7th Avenue
Suite 310
Little Rock, AR 72202
(501) 371-2603

CALIFORNIA
Department of Alcohol and Drug
    Abuse
111 Capitol Mall
Sacramento, CA 95814
(916) 445-1940

COLORADO
Department of Health
Alcohol and Drug Abuse Division
4210 East 11th Avenue
Denver, CO 80220
(303) 320-6137

CONNECTICUT
Alcohol and Drug Abuse
    Commission
999 Asylum Avenue
3rd Floor
Hartford, CT 06105
(203) 566-4145

DELAWARE
Division of Mental Health
Bureau of Alcoholism and Drug
    Abuse
1901 North Dupont Highway
Newcastle, DE 19720
(302) 421-6101

DISTRICT OF COLUMBIA
Department of Human Services
Office of Health Planning and
  Development
601 Indiana Avenue, NW
Suite 500
Washington, D.C. 20004
(202) 724-5641

FLORIDA
Department of Health and
  Rehabilitative Services
Alcoholic Rehabilitation Program
1317 Winewood Boulevard
Room 187A
Tallahassee, FL 32301
(904) 488-0396

Department of Health and
  Rehabilitative Services
Drug Abuse Program
1317 Winewood Boulevard
Building 6, Room 155
Tallahassee, FL 32301
(904) 488-0900

GEORGIA
Department of Human Resources
Division of Mental Health and
  Mental Retardation
Alcohol and Drug Section
618 Ponce De Leon Avenue, NE
Atlanta, GA 30365-2101
(404) 894-4785

HAWAII
Department of Health
Mental Health Division
Alcohol and Drug Abuse Branch
1250 Punch Bowl Street
P.O. Box 3378
Honolulu, HI 96801
(808) 548-4280

IDAHO
Department of Health and Welfare
Bureau of Preventive Medicine
Substance Abuse Section
450 West State
Boise, ID 83720
(208) 334-4368

ILLINOIS
Department of Mental Health and
  Developmental Disabilities
Division of Alcoholism
160 North La Salle Street
Room 1500
Chicago, IL 60601
(312) 793-2907

Illinois Dangerous Drugs
  Commission
300 North State Street
Suite 1500
Chicago, IL 60610
(312) 822-9860

INDIANA
Department of Mental Health
Division of Addiction Services
429 North Pennsylvania Street
Indianapolis, IN 46204
(317) 232-7816

IOWA
Department of Substance Abuse
505 5th Avenue
Insurance Exchange Building
Suite 202
Des Moines, IA 50319
(515) 281-3641

KANSAS
Department of Social Rehabilitation
Alcohol and Drug Abuse Services
2700 West 6th Street
Biddle Building
Topeka, KS 66606
(913) 296-3925

KENTUCKY
Cabinet for Human Resources
Department of Health Services
Substance Abuse Branch
275 East Main Street
Frankfort, KY 40601
(502) 564-2880

LOUISIANA
Department of Health and Human
  Resources
Office of Mental Health and
  Substance Abuse
655 North 5th Street
P.O. Box 4049
Baton Rouge, LA 70821
(504) 342-2565

MAINE
Department of Human Services
Office of Alcoholism and Drug
  Abuse Prevention
Bureau of Rehabilitation
32 Winthrop Street
Augusta, ME 04330
(207) 289-2781

MARYLAND
Alcoholism Control Administration
201 West Preston Street
Fourth Floor
Baltimore, MD 21201
(301) 383-2977

State Health Department
Drug Abuse Administration
201 West Preston Street
Baltimore, MD 21201
(301) 383-3312

MASSACHUSETTS
Department of Public Health
Division of Alcoholism
755 Boylston Street
Sixth Floor
Boston, MA 02116
(617) 727-1960

Department of Public Health
Division of Drug Rehabilitation
600 Washington Street
Boston, MA 02114
(617) 727-8617

MICHIGAN
Department of Public Health
Office of Substance Abuse Services
3500 North Logan Street
P.O. Box 30035
Lansing, MI 48909
(517) 373-8603

MINNESOTA
Department of Public Welfare
Chemical Dependency Program
  Division
Centennial Building
658 Cedar Street
4th Floor
Saint Paul, MN 55155
(612) 296-4614

MISSISSIPPI
Department of Mental Health
Division of Alcohol and Drug Abuse
1102 Robert E. Lee Building
Jackson, MS 39201
(601) 359-1297

MISSOURI
Department of Mental Health
Division of Alcoholism and Drug
  Abuse
2002 Missouri Boulevard
P.O. Box 687
Jefferson City, MO 65102
(314) 751-4942

MONTANA
Department of Institutions
Alcohol and Drug Abuse Division
1539 11th Avenue
Helena, MT 59620
(406) 449-2827

NEBRASKA
Department of Public Institutions
Division of Alcoholism and Drug
Abuse
801 West Van Dorn Street
P.O. Box 94728
Lincoln, NB 68509
(402) 471-2851, Ext. 415

NEVADA
Department of Human Resources
Bureau of Alcohol and Drug Abuse
505 East King Street
Carson City, NV 89710
(702) 885-4790

NEW HAMPSHIRE
Department of Health and Welfare
Office of Alcohol and Drug Abuse
  Prevention
Hazen Drive
Health and Welfare Building
Concord, NH 03301
(603) 271-4627

NEW JERSEY
Department of Health
Division of Alcoholism
129 East Hanover Street CN 362
Trenton, NJ 08625
(609) 292-8949

Department of Health
Division of Narcotic and Drug
  Abuse Control
129 East Hanover Street CN 362
Trenton, NJ 08625
(609) 292-8949

NEW MEXICO
Health and Environment Department
Behavioral Services Division
Substance Abuse Bureau
725 Saint Michaels Drive
P.O. Box 968
Santa Fe, NM 87503
(505) 984-0020, Ext. 304

NEW YORK
Division of Alcoholism and Alcohol
  Abuse
194 Washington Avenue
Albany, NY 12210
(518) 474-5417

Division of Substance Abuse
  Services
Executive Park South
Box 8200
Albany, NY 12203
(518) 457-7629

NORTH CAROLINA
Department of Human Resources
Division of Mental Health, Mental
  Retardation and Substance Abuse
  Services
Alcohol and Drug Abuse Services
325 North Salisbury Street
Albemarle Building
Raleigh, NC 27611
(919) 733-4670

NORTH DAKOTA
Department of Human Services
Division of Alcoholism and Drug
  Abuse
State Capitol Building
Bismarck, ND 58505
(701) 224-2767

OHIO
Department of Health
Division of Alcoholism
246 North High Street
P.O. Box 118
Columbus, OH 43216
(614) 466-3543

Department of Mental Health
Bureau of Drug Abuse
65 South Front Street
Columbus, OH 43215
(614) 466-9023

OKLAHOMA
Department of Mental Health
Alcohol and Drug Programs
4545 North Lincoln Boulevard
Suite 100 East Terrace
P.O. Box 53277
Oklahoma City, OK 73152
(405) 521-0044

OREGON
Department of Human Resources
Mental Health Division
Office of Programs for Alcohol and
  Drug Problems
2575 Bittern Street, NE
Salem, OR 97310
(503) 378-2163

PENNSYLVANIA
Department of Health
Office of Drug and Alcohol
  Programs
Commonwealth and Forster Avenues
Health and Welfare Building
P.O. Box 90
Harrisburg, PA 17108
(717) 787-9857

RHODE ISLAND
Department of Mental Health,
  Mental Retardation and Hospitals
Division of Substance Abuse
Substance Abuse Administration
  Building
Cranston, RI 02920
(401) 464-2091

SOUTH CAROLINA
Commission on Alcohol and Drug
  Abuse
3700 Forest Drive
Columbia, SC 29204
(803) 758-2521

SOUTH DAKOTA
Department of Health
Division of Alcohol and Drug Abuse
523 East Capitol, Joe Foss Building
Pierre, SD 57501
(605) 773-4806

TENNESSEE
Department of Mental Health and
  Mental Retardation
Alcohol and Drug Abuse Services
505 Deaderick Street
James K. Polk Building,
  Fourth Floor
Nashville, TN 37219
(615) 741-1921

TEXAS
Commission on Alcoholism
809 Sam Houston State Office
  Building
Austin, TX 78701
(512) 475-2577
Department of Community Affairs
Drug Abuse Prevention Division
2015 South Interstate Highway 35
P.O. Box 13166
Austin, TX 78711
(512) 443-4100

UTAH
Department of Social Services
Division of Alcoholism and Drugs
150 West North Temple
Suite 350
P.O. Box 2500
Salt Lake City, UT 84110
(801) 533-6532

VERMONT
Agency of Human Services
Department of Social and
  Rehabilitation Services
Alcohol and Drug Abuse Division
103 South Main Street
Waterbury, VT 05676
(802) 241-2170

VIRGINIA
Department of Mental Health and
  Mental Retardation
Division of Substance Abuse
109 Governor Street
P.O. Box 1797
Richmond, VA 23214
(804) 786-5313

WASHINGTON
Department of Social and Health
  Service
Bureau of Alcohol and Substance
  Abuse
Office Building—44 W
Olympia, WA 98504
(206) 753-5866

WEST VIRGINIA
Department of Health
Office of Behavioral Health Services
Division on Alcoholism and Drug
  Abuse
1800 Washington Street East
Building 3 Room 451
Charleston, WV 25305
(304) 348-2276

WISCONSIN
Department of Health and Social
  Services
Division of Community Services
Bureau of Community Programs
Alcohol and Other Drug Abuse
  Program Office
1 West Wilson Street
P.O. Box 7851
Madison, WI 53707
(608) 266-2717

WYOMING
Alcohol and Drug Abuse Programs
Hathaway Building
Cheyenne, WY 82002
(307) 777-7115, Ext. 7118

GUAM
Mental Health & Substance Abuse
  Agency
P.O. Box 20999
Guam 96921

PUERTO RICO
Department of Addiction Control
  Services
Alcohol Abuse Programs
P.O. Box B-Y Rio Piedras Station
Rio Piedras, PR 00928
(809) 763-5014

Department of Addiction Control
  Services
Drug Abuse Programs
P.O. Box B-Y Rio Piedras Station
Rio Piedras, PR 00928
(809) 764-8140

VIRGIN ISLANDS
Division of Mental Health,
  Alcoholism & Drug Dependency
  Services
P.O. Box 7329
Saint Thomas, Virgin Islands 00801
(809) 774-7265

AMERICAN SAMOA
LBJ Tropical Medical Center
Department of Mental Health Clinic
Pago Pago, American Samoa 96799

TRUST TERRITORIES
Director of Health Services
Office of the High Commissioner
Saipan, Trust Territories 96950

Further Reading

Fromme, M.; Kagen, D.; and Stone, N. *Cocaine: Seduction and Solution*. New York: Clarkson N. Potter, 1984.

Gold, M. S. *800-Cocaine*. New York: Bantam Books, 1984.

Meryman, Richard. *Broken Promises, Mended Dreams*. Boston: Little, Brown, 1984.

Narcotics Anonymous. Van Nuys, California: World Services Inc., 1984.

Seixas, J., and Youcha, G. *Children of Alcoholism*. New York: Crown Publishers, 1985.

Woodward, N. *If Your Child is Drinking*. New York: G. P. Putnam's Sons, 1981.

Glossary

abstinence voluntary refrainment from the use of alcohol and/or other drugs

addiction a condition caused by repeated drug use, characterized by a compulsive urge to continue using the drug, a tendency to increase the dosage, and physiological and/or psychological dependence

alcoholism alcohol abuse causing deterioration in health and social relations

amphetamine any one of a number of drugs that act to stimulate parts of the central nervous system

barbiturates any one of a number of drugs that cause depression of the central nervous system, generally used to reduce anxiety or induce euphoria

blackout temporary loss of consciousness

bulimia condition in which extreme hunger is experienced shortly after ingesting a meal

cocaine the primary psychoactive ingredient in the coca plant; it functions as a behavioral stimulant

cold turkey the process of withdrawing suddenly and without the help of therapeutic aids from a highly addictive drug

crack a less expensive, highly addictive form of cocaine

detoxification the body's process for removing poisonous substances or rendering them harmless; the liver is often employed to perform this function

flashback the return of hallucinogenic images after the immediate effects of hallucinogens have worn off

freebasing a potent and dangerous method whereby street cocaine is mixed with ammonium hydroxide and heated, then smoked in a pipe for a quick and addictive high

hallucinogen a drug that produces sensory impressions that have no basis in reality

heroin a semisynthetic opiate produced by a chemical modification of morphine

lysergic acid diethylamide a hallucinogenic drug derived from a fungus that grows on rye or from morning-glory seeds

narcotic originally a group of drugs producing effects similar to those of morphine; often used to refer to any substance that sedates, has a depressive effect, and/or causes dependence

opiate any compound from the milky juice of the poppy plant *Papaver somniferum*, including opium, morphine, codeine, and heroin

outpatient a patient who receives medical, psychiatric, or therapeutic treatment on a routine basis at a medical center but who lives at home and participates in many of the regular routines of his or her daily life

overdose a large quantity of a drug taken accidentally or on purpose, which causes temporary or permanent damage to the body and may be fatal

paranoia a tendency to suspect and mistrust others to the extreme

phencyclidine also known as PCP or angel dust; a potent preparation that is mixed with other drugs to enhance their effects, it can produce dangerous and terrifying hallucinations or psychotic reactions

physical dependence an adaptation of the body to the presence of a drug such that its absence produces withdrawal symptoms

psychoactive altering mood and/or behavior

psychological dependence a condition in which the drug user craves a drug to maintain a sense of well-being and feels discomfort when deprived of it

rehabilitation training that enables a person to return to and function in daily life after a period of imprisonment or illness

side effects desirable or undesirable results of the use of a drug in addition to the intended result

therapeutic having medicinal or healing properties

tolerance a decrease of susceptibility to the effects of a drug due to its continued administration, resulting in the user's need to increase the drug dosage in order to achieve the effects experienced previously

withdrawal the physiological and psychological effects of discontinued use of a drug

Picture Credits

AP/Wide World Photos: pp. 57, 59, 60; Art Resource: p. 6; The Bettmann Archive: p. 12; Ann Chwatsky/Art Resource: p. 10; Courtesy of Fair Oaks Hospital: p. 60; Courtesy of Phoenix House: pp. 8, 59; UPI/Bettmann Newsphotos: pp. 56, 58, 62, 63

Index

Dianne Hales is a freelance writer specializing in medical topics and the author of *An Invitation to Health.* She is also a contributing editor for *American Health* magazine.

Solomon H. Snyder, M.D. is Distinguished Service Professor of Neuroscience, Pharmacology and Psychiatry at The Johns Hopkins University School of Medicine. He has served as president of the Society for Neuroscience and in 1978 received the Albert Lasker Award in Medical Research. He has authored *Uses of Marijuana, Madness and the Brain, The Troubled Mind, Biological Aspects of Mental Disorder,* and edited *Perspective in Neuropharmacology: A Tribute to Julius Axelrod.* Professor Snyder was a research associate with Dr. Axelrod at the National Institutes of Health.

Barry L. Jacobs, Ph.D., is currently a professor in the program of neuroscience at Princeton University. Professor Jacobs is author of *Serotonin Neurotransmission and Behavior* and *Hallucinogens: Neurochemical, Behavioral and Clinical Perspectives.* He has written many journal articles in the field of neuroscience and contributed numerous chapters to books on behavior and brain science. He has been a member of several panels of the National Institute of Mental Health.

Joann Ellison Rodgers, M.S. (Columbia), became Deputy Director of Public Affairs and Director of Media Relations for the Johns Hopkins Medical Institutions in Baltimore, Maryland, in 1984 after 18 years as an award-winning science journalist and widely read columnist for the Hearst newspapers.